PRAISE FOR
The Magdeburg Confession: With Historical Introduction and Annotations

The Magdeburg Confession takes the question of authority seriously: it is no rationalization of insubordination nor of avoiding crosses that Christ may send our way. Rather, it reminds us that Christ preserves and extends His kingdom through means—not only the means of grace but also vocations such as minister, father, and magistrate. Preus and MacPherson's new translation and commentary impress upon us again the importance of the scriptural doctrine of vocation: those who hold authoritative offices have the duty and the joy of advocating for what is good and right, what supports and extends the Gospel.

Gifford Grobien
The David P. Scaer Professor of Biblical and Systematic Theology, Concordia Theological Seminary, Fort Wayne, Indiana

At a time in which confessional Lutheranism is assailed on all sides, the courageously faithful response of nine principled Lutheran pastors to the Augsburg Interim and imposition of Roman Catholicism reads today like a clarion call to orthodoxy come what may. The Magdeburg Confession was itself a line in the sand to tyrannical imposition. May contemporary readers find similar inspiration to stand for Christ's Word and our holy faith.

Commander Rev. John J. Bombaro, PhD
Senior Pastor, St. James Lutheran Church, Lafayette, Indiana
US Navy Reserve Chaplain

Lutheran leaders in the sixteenth century had to use both diplomacy and military power to carve out a place for the Reformation to flourish. In 1550, with a hostile army outside its walls, Magdeburg's leaders and ministers confessed that at times civil disobedience and even armed resistance are necessary to preserve the Gospel. While this "confession" was never accepted as an official confession of the Lutheran Church outside of that city, the arguments made in the Magdeburg Confession are important for Christians today who must face, at some times and in some places, persecutions similar to those of 1550.

Benjamin T. G. Mayes
Associate Professor of Historical Theology
Concordia Theological Seminary, Fort Wayne, Indiana
Co-General Editor, *Luther's Works*: American Edition

The Magdeburg Confession

With Historical Introduction and Annotations

TRANSLATED BY
CHRISTIAN PREUS

INTRODUCED BY
RYAN C. MACPHERSON

CONCORDIA PUBLISHING HOUSE • SAINT LOUIS

Copyright © 2025 Concordia Publishing House
3558 S. Jefferson Ave., St. Louis, MO 63118-3968
1-800-325-3040 • cph.org

Unless otherwise indicated, quotations from Scripture and other authors have been translated from the original.

Manufactured in the United States of America

1 2 3 4 5 6 7 8 9 10 34 33 32 31 30 29 28 27 26 25

CONTENTS

TRANSLATOR'S PREFACE

THE Magdeburg Confession was written in both Latin and German, but, as with the Augsburg Confession, the one is not a translation of the other. Instead, the German says essentially the same thing as the Latin, but with many and free variations. While the German is referenced at times in footnotes, especially where it aids in understanding the Latin text, this translation is based on the Latin, originally published on April 13, 1550. I have followed the text of the critical edition contained in *Der Adiaphoristische Streit (1548–1560)*, the second volume of *Controversia et Confessio: Theologische Kontroversen 1548–1577/80*, edited by Irene Dingel.[1]

The original text is straightforward and to the point, written in a style that expresses the urgency of the situation. With no time for rhetorical flourishes and high style, both the pathos and logos of the confession press on the reader with immediacy. I have tried to capture this style in the English.

This is the second translation in the English language. The translation by Matthew Colvin served well to bring the Magdeburg Confession into the public eye.[2] Like many first translations, it is sometimes difficult to follow and contains translating errors, some significant. More important, perhaps, our new translation includes an introduction to provide historical and theological context, especially the interaction of this document with the Augsburg Confession and the ways in which its authors portray the Augsburg Interim as overturning the Augsburg Confession.

---

1 "Magdeburger Bekenntnis, lateinisch und deutsch (Magdeburg 1550)," ed. Hans-Otto Schneider, in *Der Adiaphoristische Streit (1548–1560)*, vol. 2 of *Controversia et Confessio: Theologische Kontroversen 1548–1577/80*, ed. Irene Dingel (Göttingen: Vandenhoeck & Ruprecht, 2012).

2 Matthew Colvin, trans., *The Magdeburg Confession: 13th of April, 1550 AD* (North Charleston, SC: CreateSpace, 2012).

Annotations in the text of the Magdeburg Confession are provided to help the reader understand biblical and historical allusions and references. Where the biblical text appears in the Latin text itself, whether in-text or in the marginalia, the biblical reference appears in-text. All other biblical references are included in the annotations. The equivalent page numbers in the Latin text are printed at the top of the page and approximate page breaks are marked with a stroke (|).

My hope is that this presentation of the Magdeburg Confession will widen the readership of this important work and encourage continued theological and historical conversation and study of the interface between the divine institutions of civil government, the household, and the Christian Church.

Soli Deo Gloria
Christian A. Preus
Feast of the Ascension, 2024

ABBREVIATIONS

For the Magdeburg Confession

The following citation conventions are provided for the Magdeburg Confession to aid the reader in internal cross-references within this volume.

MC Syl	Magdeburg Confession, Syllogism
MC Pref	Magdeburg Confession, Preface
MC CA	Magdeburg Confession, Chief Articles
MC Def	Magdeburg Confession, Defense
MC Exh	Magdeburg Confession, Exhortation
MC Post	Magdeburg Confession, Postscript

Additional Works Cited

AC	Augsburg Confession.
AE	Luther, Martin. *Luther's Works*. American Edition. Vols. 1–30: Edited by Jaroslav Pelikan. St. Louis: Concordia Publishing House, 1955–76. Vols. 31–55: Edited by Helmut Lehmann. Philadelphia/Minneapolis: Muhlenberg/Fortress, 1957–86. Vols. 56–82: Edited by Christopher Boyd Brown and Benjamin T. G. Mayes. St. Louis: Concordia Publishing House, 2009–.
Ap	Apology of the Augsburg Confession.
AS	*Der Adiaphoristische Streit (1548–1660)*. Vol. 2 of *Controversia et Confessio: Theologische Kontroversen 1548–1577/80*. Edited by Irene Dingel. Göttingen: Vandenhoeck & Ruprecht, 2012.
BoC	*The Book of Concord: The Confessions of the Evangelical Lutheran Church*. Edited by Robert Kolb and Timothy J. Wengert. Minneapolis: Fortress Press, 2000.

Concordia	*Concordia: The Lutheran Confessions.* 2nd ed. St. Louis: Concordia Publishing House, 2006.
CR	*Corpus Reformatorum: Philippi Melanchthonis Opera quae supersunt Omnia.* 28 vols. Edited by C. G. Bretschneider. Halle: Schwetschke, 1834–60.
Denzinger	Heinrich Denzinger, ed. *Enchiridion symbolorum definitionum et declarationum de rebus fidei et morum.* 34th ed. Edited by Adolf Schönmetzer. Freiburg: Herder, 1967. Cited according to the numbering at http://denzinger.patristica.net.
FC	Formula of Concord.
FC Ep	Epitome of the Formula of Concord.
LC	Large Catechism.
LSB	The Commission on Worship of The Lutheran Church—Missouri Synod. *Lutheran Service Book.* St. Louis: Concordia Publishing House, 2006.
NPNF[1]	*A Select Library of the Christian Church: Nicene and Post-Nicene Fathers: First Series.* Edited by Philip Schaff. 14 vols. New York, 1886–89. Reprint, Peabody, MA: Hendrickson, 1994.
NPNF[2]	*A Select Library of the Christian Church: Nicene and Post-Nicene Fathers: Second Series.* Edited by Philip Schaff and Henry Wace. 14 vols. New York, 1890–1900. Reprint, Peabody, MA: Hendrickson, 1994.
SC	*Sources and Contexts of The Book of Concord.* Edited by Robert Kolb and James A. Nestingen. Minneapolis: Fortress Press, 2001.
WA	*D. Martin Luthers Werke: Kritische Gesamtausgabe.* 73 vols. Weimar: Hermann Böhlau, 1930–.

INTRODUCTION TO THE
Magdeburg Confession

Ryan C. MacPherson

THE HISTORICAL CONTEXT OF THE MAGDEBURG CONFESSION

ON the Ides of April 1550—April 13—a dying man in the German city of Magdeburg insisted that his signature appear on a document, a formal protest against pope, emperor, and Satan alike. While the exact details may be difficult to pin down, an early printing of that document, the Magdeburg Confession, bears the date "Anno 1550 Idibus Aprilis" on the frontispiece and is appended with an identically dated note concerning Stephanus Tucher's final wishes.[1] His friends stated: "When we came to visit him as he struggled with his sickness, some of us heard him very firmly and indignantly condemn the deceits of the Interimists and Adiaphorists. . . . They heard him also exhort us to persevere in this our true confession against the contagion of that Pharisaical leaven."[2]

Why was it so important that Tucher sign this document? What deceits were he and his friends so concerned about that they were willing to take on the highest civil and religious authorities in the middle years of the sixteenth century? While some Christians today may connect the mention of "Pharisaical leaven" to the accusations

---

1 Tucher had attained a master's degree in liberal arts at the University of Wittenberg on February 9, 1542, under Joachim Rheticus, Wittenberg's leading mathematician (see Julius Köstlin, ed., *Die Baccalaurei und Magistri der Wittenberger Philosophiscen Facultät, 1538–1546 und die Öffentlichen Disputationen derselben Jahre aus der Facultatätsmatrikel* [Halle: Osterprogramm der Universität Halle-Wittenberg, 1890], 13). In 1544, Tucher was admitted into the collegiate faculty (Köstlin, *Die Baccalaurei und Magistri*, 22). Within a few years, all that his former Wittenberg professors had stood for as Lutherans was under attack, but only some of those professors were willing to rise to defend the faith. By 1550, the last bastion of Lutheranism, Magdeburg, was under siege. As Tucher worried that he would not live to sign the final draft of the Magdeburg Confession, he urged local pastors to sign on his behalf.

2 See below, MC Post, p. 125.

of works-righteousness leveled against Papists by the followers of Martin Luther, fewer people may know of the 1548 Augsburg Interim, the subsequent Leipzig Interim, or the Adiaphoristic Controversy that arose as a result. The Magdeburgers' words and actions would influence John Knox's reformation of Scotland, be applied to justify the execution of King Charles I in England, and also shape the thinking of John Adams and other patriots in the American colonies. Today, the Magdeburg Confession still has much to say concerning how Christians live in their various vocations in the household, in civil society, and in the church.

Magdeburg: A Center of Lutheran Liberty

Niccolò Machiavelli exaggerated, but only slightly, when writing in *The Prince* (ca. 1513) that "the cities of Germany are completely free . . . obey the emperor when they want to, and they do not fear him or any other neighboring power."[3] Even if not "completely free," the German principalities did enjoy a long-standing heritage that prized local liberty: German warriors halted the expansion of Rome in the Battle of Teutoburg Forest (AD 9) and the early-second-century Roman historian Tacitus found their "freedom of spirit" remarkable.[4] The Lutheran Reformation, which redirected people's loyalties to local pastors preaching Scripture, to local princes protecting their churches, and to local families living ordinary vocations to the glory of God and for the good of their neighbors, took root in German soil in part because Luther, with such a message, "was the most German German of them all."[5] By the 1540s, the recurring rhetorical association of Lutheran grace with "German liberty" shaped the Saxon psyche to view the Reformation as both a blessing and a responsibility in the special charge of local pastors who, in turn, sought the protection of their regional princes or local magistrates. The preservation of true doctrine required temporal and ecclesiastical leaders each to

3 Niccolò Machiavelli, *The Prince*, chap. 10, in *The Prince and Other Writings*, trans. Wayne Rebhorn (New York: Barnes & Noble Classics, 2003), 46.

4 John Eidsmoe, *Historical and Theological Foundations of Law*, 2nd ed., 3 vols. (Ventura, CA: Nordskog, 2016), 2:795–804.

5 Will Durant, *The Reformation: A History of European Civilization from Wyclif to Calvin, 1300–1564*, The Story of Civilization 6 (New York: Simon & Schuster, 1957), 453.

stand guard against Satan, the papacy, and—at times—the emperor as well.[6]

Within the German landscape, Magdeburg stood out in the sixteenth century.[7] Once the capital of Otto the Great (Holy Roman emperor, r. 962–973), and also claiming *Altfreiheit* (ancient liberties) from the pre-Ottonian era, Magdeburg enjoyed a rich, if complicated, history of ordered liberty. Magdeburg styled itself *reichsfreie und kaiserliche*, meaning that the City Council considered itself on par with the imperial electors. The city was not to be ruled by the pope, and it would submit to the emperor only in matters in which the emperor had jurisdiction—certainly not in any ecclesiastical matters.[8]

The Lutheran faith came to Magdeburg first through song. Even before the reformer himself set foot in the town, two of his hymns were sung in May 1524. "Out of the Depths I Cry to Thee" instructed the people that upon the confession of their sins, they should expect to hear Christ's absolution, or full forgiveness, solely by God's grace alone, without any need of penance or works of satisfaction on their part.[9] "May God Bestow on Us His Grace," as the title itself makes plain, emphasized similar themes.[10] Among Luther's first four published hymns, these two were part of the repertoire sung at Mass in Magdeburg before the sermon. As a result, the Roman Catholic service was becoming Lutheran. Authorities friendly to the pope had the itinerant peddler of Luther's hymns imprisoned for causing a public disturbance, but a gathering of about seven hundred townspeople at St. John's Parish on May 6 stood ready to liberate him by force, if necessary.[11]

---

6 For the development of "German liberty" as a rhetorical trope among early Lutherans, see Nathan Rein, *The Chancery of God: Protestant Print, Polemic and Propaganda against the Empire, Magdeburg, 1546–1551* (Hampshire: Ashgate, 2008), ch. 2. Rein concludes that German Lutheran exceptionalism was one of the five most significant "maxims" shaping the self-understanding of Magdeburg's pamphleteers during the Interim Controversy (see *Chancery of God*, 204–6).

7 Rein, *Chancery of God*, 9–15.

8 Rein, *Chancery of God*, 11, 59–60.

9 See "From Depths of Woe I Cry to Thee," *LSB* 607.

10 See *LSB* 823/824.

11 J. Andreas Loewe, "Why Do Lutherans Sing? Lutherans, Music, and the Gospel in the First Century of the Reformation," *Church History* 82, no. 1 (2013): 69–89.

Seven weeks later, on June 26, 1524, Luther himself preached at St. John's on the theme of true and false righteousness. St. John's stood near the *Rathaus* (municipal building) in the *Altstadt*, or old quarter of the city, which was not under the jurisdiction of Cardinal-Archbishop Albert of Magdeburg (r. 1513–45) and Mainz (r. 1514–45). Accompanying Luther on this trip was his close friend and fellow reformer in Wittenberg Nicolaus von Amsdorf. At Luther's suggestion, Amsdorf was called to St. Ulrich's in Magdeburg, though political complications initially dissuaded him from accepting. If Amsdorf were to serve in Magdeburg, he would lose the protection of Elector Frederick the Wise of Saxony and would be at the mercy of Cardinal-Archbishop Albert, Elector Frederick's rival in imperial politics and a staunch supporter of the papacy. To finance his own acquisition of ecclesiastical titles, Albert had sponsored Johann Tetzel's sale of indulgences, opposition to which had brought Luther into the public eye several years earlier.[12]

With kinship, theology, and politics so delicately balanced, Frederick the Wise leveraged a minor technicality to the Reformation's advantage. He granted Amsdorf a leave of absence from residency at the University of Wittenberg, which allowed Amsdorf to remain a subject of electoral Saxony as Frederick's sponsored professor at Wittenberg even while sojourning in Magdeburg. Thus on September 24, 1524, Amsdorf became pastor at St. Ulrich's in Magdeburg and also superintendent of the city's churches.[13] An able polemicist, he challenged Albert's theologians to a public disputation and, when they refused to appear, published tracts demonstrating the dangerous errors of papal teachings while also warning against the errors of the Anabaptists and Zwinglians.[14] Amsdorf's recurring themes would appear again in the Magdeburg Confession: Christians must avoid the spiritual and secular tyranny of the papacy, as well as the chaotic anarchy of the Anabaptists, who deny the means of grace by rejecting the sacraments and also reject God's means of temporal justice by rejecting lawful civil ordinances.

---

12 Diarmaid MacCulloch, *The Reformation: A History* (New York: Penguin, 2003), 121.

13 Robert Kolb, *Nikolaus von Amsdorf: Champion of Martin Luther's Reformation* (St. Louis: Concordia Publishing House, 2019), 19.

14 Kolb, *Nikolaus von Amsdorf*, 22–29.

The Rise and Fall of the Smalcaldic League

As papal and imperial powers attempted to stem the Reformation, leaders throughout the German territories and cities considered ways to maintain Lutheran orthodoxy while honoring God's call of obedience to those in authority over them. On June 26, 1526, the City Council made Magdeburg's *Rathaus* available for the organizing meeting of what would become the League of Magdeburg, a confederation of Lutheran principalities. But from the perspective of Holy Roman Emperor Charles V (r. 1519–56), Lutherans were, like the radicals who had fomented the Peasants' War of 1524–25, a dangerous and meddlesome group that hindered unity in a Christian empire that was struggling to stand against the Turks. Thus did Dr. Johann Eck caricature Luther in his *404 Propositions* (1530). In a cover letter to the emperor, Eck called Luther "*hostis ecclesiae domesticus*," a domestic enemy of the church.[15]

To counteract this smear campaign, Philip Melanchthon, one of Luther's fellow professors at the University of Wittenberg, synthesized Luther's writings into a defense and confession: the Augsburg Confession. This document was presented to Charles at the imperial diet in Augsburg on June 25, 1530. Eck's party produced *A Response to the Augsburg Confession*, which the Lutherans promptly renamed the *Papal Confutation*. Charles gave the Lutherans until April 15, 1531, to accept the *Confutation* and amend their ways. Instead, Melanchthon accused Rome's theologians of fallacious reasoning and defended the Lutheran doctrine on the basis of Holy Scripture, church history, and plain logic in the Apology of the Augsburg Confession (1531).[16]

Meanwhile, the Lutheran princes realized they might need arms as much as words to defend themselves. Luther initially hesitated to contemplate the use of force against an unjust ruler. The recent Peasants' War had caused more problems than it had solved, and Luther also desired to distinguish his own theology from that of the radical preacher Thomas Müntzer, who had instigated that uprising.

---

15 Quoting Friedrich Bente, "Historical Introductions to the Symbolical Books of the Evangelical Lutheran Church," in *Triglot Concordia: The Symbolical Books of the Evangelical Lutheran Church* (St. Louis: Concordia Publishing House, 1921), 16; see also Clyde L. Manschreck, *Melanchthon: The Quiet Reformer* (Nashville: Abingdon, 1958), 179–80.

16 Bente, "Historical Introductions," 17–43. See below, p. 28 n. 4, for examples of Melanchthon's identifications of logical fallacies in Rome's argumentation.

In a meeting at Torgau, however, experts in imperial law clarified that Charles did not hold his power absolutely; rather, because he was chosen by electors, the electors had the authority to keep his power in check. The Torgau Declaration of 1530 provided a theoretical foundation for the Smalcaldic League that formed in 1531, of which Magdeburg was a charter member.[17] The Lutheran princes and other leaders in the league pledged themselves to protect one another as they together protected the Lutheran churches within their realms. In response, Charles V revoked Magdeburg's status as a "free imperial city."[18] Nearly a decade later, in 1539, Luther together with Justus Jonas, Martin Bucer, and Philip Melanchthon concluded furthermore that not merely a reactive defense but even a preemptive defense may permissibly be waged by secular leaders against papal or imperial forces that would threaten the Lutheran churches.[19]

Following Luther's death in February 1546, Charles V expected that, if threatened, the reformer's followers would lose heart. A truce with the Turks, concluded in 1547, left the empire secure against threats from the outside and therefore less dependent upon the Lutheran territories for military assistance.[20] For the imperial forces, the timing seemed right for a military intervention to restore the order Charles sought in church and state. However, when united, the Smalcaldic League could mobilize more troops in Saxony than could the emperor.[21] Therefore, Charles sought to drive a wedge between the league's members. To do so, he took advantage of a political situation from 1543, when the emperor had extended immunity to

---

17 Oliver K. Olson, "Theology of Revolution: Magdeburg, 1550–1551," *The Sixteenth Century Journal* 3, no. 1 (1972): 56–79, here at pp. 62–67.

18 David Mark Whitford, *Tyranny and Resistance: The Magdeburg Confession and the Lutheran Tradition* (St. Louis: Concordia Publishing House, 2001), 64.

19 Cynthia Grant Shoenberger, "The Development of the Lutheran Theory of Resistance: 1523–1530," *Sixteenth Century Journal* 8, no. 1 (1977): 61–76; Cynthia Grant Shoenberger, "Luther and the Justifiability of Resistance to Legitimate Authority," *Journal of the History of Ideas* 40, no. 1 (1979): 3–20; Ryan C. MacPherson, "Natural Law in the Lutheran Reformation," *Logia* 29, no. 1 (2020): 13–19, here at pp. 17–18. See also *Circular Disputation on the Right of Resistance against the Emperor* (1539), AE 72.

20 Geoffrey Parker, *Emperor: A New Life of Charles V* (New Haven, CT: Yale University Press, 2019), 512.

21 Manuel Fernández Alvarez, *Charles V: Elected Emperor and Hereditary Ruler* (London: Thames & Hudson, 1975), 132.

Philip, landgrave of Hesse, for his capital offense of bigamy. In return, Philip was to withhold military support from William, duke of Cleves, whom the emperor sought to remove from power and thus strengthen the Hapsburg Netherlands against not only the Saxons but also King Henry VIII of England, who had married William's sister Anne, who also was the sister-in-law of John Frederick, elector of Saxony.[22] To take advantage of such political complexities, Charles now decided to employ as his military commander Duke Maurice of Saxony, who had supported the emperor against William of Cleves and was desirous of his cousin John Frederick's title over Electoral Saxony.[23] That Maurice's sister was the first, and lawful, wife of Philip of Hesse added yet another dimension to the events that followed.[24]

In July 1546, a papal-imperial alliance formed, prepared to use arms to exterminate the Lutherans.[25] In November, imperial troops, funded in part by the pope[26] and led by Maurice, advanced on Wittenberg, prompting Elector John Frederick to close the university.[27] On April 24, 1547, Maurice's troops routed the Smalcaldic League at the Battle of Mühlberg, taking John Frederick captive.[28] German city after German city capitulated, including Wittenberg. In May, John Frederick was sentenced to death. Boldly refusing to renounce his Lutheran faith, he managed to have his sentence commuted in exchange for divesting his title to Duke Maurice, who then became

22 Theodore Hoyer, "The Rise and Fall of the Schmalkaldic League: The Treaty of Passau, 1552," *Concordia Theological Monthly* 23, no. 6 (1952): 401–17, here at pp. 409–10. Philip's bigamy had geopolitical, moral, and theological implications. See John Alfred Faulkner, "Luther and the Bigamous Marriage of Philip of Hesse," *The American Journal of Theology* 17, no. 2 (1913): 206–31; Manschreck, *Melanchthon*, 261–70. Regarding William of Cleves, see also Parker, *Emperor*, 262, 282–86, 294–96.

23 Alvarez, *Charles V*, 132; James D. Tracy, *Europe's Reformations, 1450–1650: Doctrine, Politics, and Community* (Lanham: Rowman & Littlefield, 2006), 142.

24 James D. Tracy, *Emperor Charles V, Impresario of War: Campaign Strategy, International Finance, and Domestic Politics* (Cambridge: Cambridge University Press, 2002), 183 n. 2.

25 Oliver K. Olson, *Matthias Flacius and the Survival of Luther's Reform* (Wiesbaden: Harrassowitz, 2002), 59.

26 Tracy, *Emperor Charles V*, 223–25.

27 Olson, *Matthias Flacius*, 68.

28 Daniel H. Nexon, *The Struggle for Power in Early Modern Europe: Religious Conflict, Dynastic Empires, and International Change* (Princeton: Princeton University Press, 2009), 176.

the ruler also of Electoral Saxony, in which Wittenberg was located, thus reuniting the two Saxonies that had been separated since 1486.[29] The other leading prince of the Smalcaldic League, Philip of Hesse, also was imprisoned for the next five years.[30]

Reaction in Magdeburg to the Augsburg and Leipzig Interims

With the Lutheran alliance shattered but military action ongoing, Charles confidently convened another diet at Augsburg (1547–48). As the diet ran its course, in April 1548 Charles V required that Lutherans celebrate the Roman Mass without any explanatory glosses. On May 15, he then pronounced the Augsburg Interim—a transitional imperial policy, pending the final action of a general church council. Although the emperor and Rome conceded that Lutherans could distribute both kinds in the Lord's Supper, Lutherans had to conform to other Roman Catholic practices that offended against the Augsburg Confession:

> The Interim linked justification to the gift of *caritas* [love], and thus to the practice of good works. It restored the power of papal bishops and the authority of the pope. It reestablished all seven medieval sacraments. It defended the medieval practice of the Mass and insisted that the Evangelicals [Lutherans] use its traditional form and trappings as well as the sacramentals which involved various areas of church life. The Interim, if enforced, spelled the end of Lutheranism.[31]

As the diet met and Maurice continued his military activities, the duke allowed the University of Wittenberg to reopen in October 1547.[32] Melanchthon urged the Lutheran remnant to accept temporary compromise measures, lest the papal-imperial alliance completely exterminate Lutheranism and close the University of Wittenberg forever. Maurice, realizing that a too-strict mandate

29 Nexon, *Struggle for Power in Early Modern Europe*, 176.

30 John E. Helmke, *Philipp of Hesse: Unlikely Hero of the Reformation* (St. Louis: Concordia Publishing House, 2018), 173–85.

31 Robert Kolb, *Andreae and the Formula of Concord: Six Sermons on the Way to Lutheran Unity* (St. Louis: Concordia Publishing House, 1977), 21.

32 Olson, *Matthias Flacius*, 73.

could lead to an uprising among the Saxon Lutherans, met with Melanchthon in Leipzig to draft a more permissive interim policy (published in December 1548). Although never authorized by Charles, it was called the "Leipzig Interim" by Matthias Flacius and other stalwart Lutherans who sought refuge in Magdeburg.[33] Among other controversies, this interim brought debate over what could be considered adiaphora (something neither forbidden nor commanded in Scripture). Convinced that submission to either interim was idolatrous before God and treasonous before their magistrates, the theologians of Magdeburg had bolder resolve. They vociferously opposed the pope, the emperor, Maurice, and Melanchthon with an arsenal of pamphlets.[34]

Flacius's party objected to political leaders meddling in theological matters and furthermore opposed Melanchthon's compromising spirit. Melanchthon believed compromise was permissible regarding indifferent matters (adiaphora), such as the details of church vestments and liturgical rituals. Flacius disagreed with his former mentor as to which details truly were indifferent. More fundamentally, he objected that in the context of a theological controversy in which one side is politically coercing the other, an otherwise indifferent matter ceases to be indifferent. Clear confession of sound doctrine requires outward worship practices that testify unambiguously to that confession. The adage *lex orandi, lex credendi* (the pattern of worship corresponds to the pattern of belief) implied, in Flacius's outlook, also *lex orandi, lex confitendi* (one's worship is an act of confessing the faith publicly).[35] Especially troubling was the Roman Catholic insistence that the Leipzig concessions were to be interpreted according to the Augsburg Interim, rather than vice versa.[36] Crying "Adiaphora!" could not transform scripturally divisive matters into adiaphora, nor could it remove actual adiaphora from the scandalous context of

---

33 On the activities of Flacius and the Magdeburgers, see Olson, *Matthias Flacius*, and Wade Johnson, *Life under the Cross: A Biography of the Reformer Matthias Flacius Illyricus* (St. Louis: Concordia Publishing House, 2025).

34 "Every historian who mentions a 'Leipzig Interim' without a hint that the term was ever controversial gives evidence of Flacius's stunning victory" in his propaganda war, as he painted the Leipzig policy as an imperial mandate to rally stronger resistance to it (Olson, *Matthias Flacius*, 127).

35 Olson, *Matthias Flacius*, 156.

36 Olson, *Matthias Flacius*, 126.

controversy that had rendered those otherwise indifferent matters properly divisive. Flacius soon published *A Book about True and False Adiaphora* to expose the dangers he saw in Melanchthon's compromises.[37] Flacius's party, claiming to represent Luther's "genuine" heritage, became known as "Gnesio-Lutherans" in contrast to the "compromising" Philippists.[38]

As Maurice's troops advanced in 1550, Magdeburg remained as the sole stronghold in the German states that refused to comply with the interim. Rejected by their former Wittenberg professors, the theologians in Magdeburg maintained an increasingly unpopular viewpoint. Even Johann Bugenhagen, Luther's own pastor, praised from the pulpit those who died digging siege works for Duke Maurice's assault against disobedient Magdeburg.[39] Within Magdeburg, clever jingles were sung and catechetical puns were developed to alert Saxony of the dangers Wittenberg's faculty had obscured:

> What is the Interim? It is an adverb [*adverbium*]. What is an adverb [*adverbium*]? It is Satan's word [*verbum*] joined with God's Word [*verbum*], so that [*ad*] souls will be deceived, the idolatry of the Antichrist will be established, and tyranny will be confirmed.[40]

As Flacius's brother-in-law[41] Stephanus Tucher urged in his posthumous epilogue to the Magdeburg Confession, faithful Christians must resist "deceits of the Interimists and Adiaphorists" at all costs.[42] Convinced that accepting the interims meant rejecting God, more than one hundred pamphlets rehearsed the theological convictions of the town's pastors and citizens and sustained their spirits during those

---

37 *Ein buch, von waren und falschen Mitteldingen, Darin fast der gantze handel von Mitteldingen erkleret wird, widder die schedliche Rotte der Adiaphoristen* (Magdeburg: Christian Rödinger, 1550). See Wade Johnston, "We Must Obey God Rather Than Men: The Lutheran Legacy of Resistance," *Logia* 25, no. 3 (2016): 19–24, here at pp. 21–23.

38 Tracy, *Europe's Reformations*, 91.

39 Olson, *Matthias Flacius*, 202.

40 Thomas Kaufmann, " 'Our Lord God's Chancery' in Magdeburg and Its Fight against the Interim," *Church History* 73, no. 3 (2004): 566–82, here at p. 578 n. 48 (Latin). The interims occupied the minds of Magdeburgers so much that even a dog was named "Interim"; see, Kaufmann, "Our Lord God's Chancery," 578.

41 Olson, *Matthias Flacius*, 150.

42 See below, MC Post, p. 125.

trying times.[43] Chief among those publications stands the Magdeburg Confession of April 13, 1550.[44]

The Magdeburg Confession

Grounded in the timeless teachings of the Scriptures and the Augsburg Confession, the Magdeburg Confession both transcended the crisis of 1550 and also provided prudent advice for that same emergency. It reaffirmed the historic Christian teachings confessed by Luther's followers at the Diet of Augsburg in 1530[45] and further articulated a theology of political resistance on the basis of Scripture, natural law, and both sacred and secular history.[46] Just as a Christian should gladly hear the pure preaching of the Gospel and gladly receive the pure administration of the Sacraments but avoid those congregations that teach or practice contrary to God's Word,[47] so also a citizen is obligated to obey civil governments that punish the evildoer and protect the innocent but resist when, in the name of civil authority, a tyrant punishes the innocent and praises the evildoer.[48] Applying a distinctively Lutheran understanding of vocation to the conflicts between the papacy and the churches of the Augsburg Confession, and between the emperor and the German princes, the Magdeburg Confession identified four levels of injustice and the appropriate remedies for each.[49] What is forbidden, what is permissible, what is prudent, and what is obligatory for a person suffering the tyranny of pope or emperor must partly depend upon that person's stations across the three estates of family, church, and civil society. In the present situation, the Magdeburgers concluded that their pastors had the sacred duty to exhort the local magistrates to stand their ground,

---

43 On the pamphlet war, see Olson, "Theology of Revolution," 70–71.

44 *Bekentnis [Bekenntnis] Vnterricht und vermanung, der Pfarrhern und Prediger, der Christlichen Kirchen zu Magdeburk anno 1550. den 13. Aprilis* (Magdeburg: M. Lotther, 1550); *Confessio et apologia pastorum & reliquorum ministrorum ecclesiæ Magdeburgensis, anno 1550. idibus Aprilis* (Magdeburg: Lotter, 1550). For other editions and translations, see below, "Recommended Reading," p. 26.

45 See below, MC CA, pp. 53–81.

46 See below, MC Def, pp. 85–108.

47 See below, MC CA, pp. 74–78.

48 See below, MC Def, p. 94.

49 See below, MC Def, pp. 95–97.

by force if necessary, against the imperial assailants, even as every head of household should devote himself to prayer and implore his rulers to act justly. Of special importance, local magistrates had both a sacred and a civil duty to interpose between the people and a tyrant abusing a higher office.[50]

Although the bulk of the 147 books and pamphlets published in the lead-up to and during the siege of Magdeburg may be traced to Flacius and his circle of Gnesio-Lutherans,[51] scholars have attributed the Magdeburg Confession variously to Nicolaus von Amsdorf and Nikolaus Gallus.[52] Matthew Colvin, the first to translate the Magdeburg Confession into English, singles out Amsdorf's pen and his sixteenth-century neo-Latin style.[53] After the text of the confession, Amsdorf's name indeed appears first, with Gallus's second, then the signatures of seven other Magdeburg pastors, each subscribing in his own hand and followed by the name of the parish he served.[54] Neither the city's leading lay theologian, Matthias Flacius, nor any pastors from beyond Magdeburg who were temporarily seeking refuge in the city signed the document.[55] Only those who held divine calls to serve as pastors in the city bore the responsibility to affix their signatures. Amsdorf's

50 See below, MC Exh, pp. 109–23.

51 Olson, "Theology of Revolution," 70–71.

52 The anonymous author of the Magdeburg Confession "certo altri non poteva essere che Niclas Amsdorff o Nikolaus Gallus" ["certainly could not have been other than Nicolaus (von) Amsdorf or Nikolaus Gallus"] (Merio Scattola, "Diritto Naturale e Dirito di Resistenza nella polemistica Luterana di Metà Cinquecento," *Kritische Zeitschrift für Überkonfessionelles Kirchenrecht* 2 [2015]: 83–108, here at p. 105).

53 "Translator's Preface," in *The Magdeburg Confession*, xxvii; cf. pp. x, 87, and several footnotes, *passim*. Amsdorf is also credited with authorship by Esther Hildebrand, "The Magdeburg Bekenntnis as a Possible Link between German and English Resistance Theories in the Sixteenth Century," *Archiv für Reformationsgeschichte* 71 (1980): 227–53, here at p. 234.

54 "Lucas Rosenthal, Johann Stengel, Henning Freden, Ambrose Hitfeld, Johann Baumgarten, Joachim Wolterstorp, and Henrich Gercken"; see below, p. 124. Colvin mistranslated "in nova civitate" (Latin text) as "in our city" (*The Magdeburg Confession*, 87; cf. *Confessio et Apologia Pastorum et Reliquorum ministrorum Ecclesiae Magdeburgensis*), as if the last signer represented the town as a whole. The German text reads "in der neuen Stadt," thus "in New City," corresponding to *Neustadt*, a specific district of Magdeburg. Reference to *Neustadt* was itself a jab against Rome, because already in 1545 the City Council had refused to swear allegiance to newly elected Archbishop John Albert (Olson, "Theology of Revolution," 62, 65–66).

55 Whitford, *Tyranny and Resistance*, 118 n. 3.

name, like John Hancock's upon the Declaration of Independence, stands out, but most likely because of his status as Magdeburg's first Lutheran pastor and as the Lutheran bishop of Naumberg.

Although Flacius no doubt highly influenced the content (as the confession itself affirms), one of his close companions in the Gnesio-Lutheran cause, Johann Wigand, wrote a gloss in one copy of the Magdeburg Confession identifying Gallus as the author.[56] A strong consensus of scholarship concurs that Gallus, not Amsdorf, was the chief writer.[57] Just as Melanchthon's "authorship" of the Augsburg Confession consisted of synthesizing and polishing earlier writings by Luther and his close associates,[58] so also Gallus's role should best be understood in cooperation with Amsdorf, Flacius, and others of their circle.[59] The resulting confessions of 1530 and 1550 were written neither by nor for any particular man, but rather these confessions stand as the voice of the church—neither treatises nor disputations nor commentaries, but *confessions*.

To publish, as much as to author, the Magdeburg Confession was in 1550 an act of treason. On January 10 and again on June 26, 1549, Duke Maurice had issued an edict of censorship.[60] Wittenberg obeyed. Only in Magdeburg were protests against Charles V's religious policies published.[61] Michael Lotter, son of Luther's Leipzig printer Melchior Lotter, operated the most important press in Magdeburg. He and the former Wittenberg printer Christian Rödinger, who had relocated to Magdeburg in 1540, focused on Wittenberg authors and, amid the

56 Olson, "Theology of Revolution," 67 n. 49.

57 Robert Kolb, review of *Nikolaus Gallus: Ein Beitrag zur Reformationsgeschichte der nachlutherishen Zeit*, by Hartmut Voit, *Sixteenth Century Journal* 10, no. 2 (1979): 117; Oliver K. Olson, "Matthias Flacius Illyricus, 1520–1575," in *Shapers of Religious Traditions in Germany, Switzerland, and Poland, 1560–1600*, ed. Jill Raitt (New Haven: Yale University Press, 1981), 4; Robert Kolb, *Luther's Wittenberg World: The Reformer's Family, Friends, Followers, and Foes* (Minneapolis: Fortress Press, 2018), 193; David M. Whitford, "John Adams, John Ponet, and a Lutheran Influence on the American Revolution," *Lutheran Quarterly* 15 (2001): 143–57, here at p. 143.

58 Bente, "Historical Introductions," 17–19.

59 Referring to the author(s) as "Gallus, Amsdorff, and the other Gnesio-Lutheran pastors" aptly captures the communal effort (J. Michael Raley, "Martin Luther on the Legitimacy of Resisting the Emperor," *Journal of Law and Religion* 37 [2022]: 96–132, here at p. 121).

60 Olson, *Matthias Flacius*, 124–27.

61 Kaufmann, "Our Lord God's Chancery," 568.

Adiaphoristic Controversy that followed the interims, on Wittenberg exiles such as Matthias Flacius and Nikolaus Gallus.[62] Flacius, a lay theologian without a parish call, spread his influence by working as a supervisor in Lotter's shop.[63] Even as printing output fell by more than half within the Holy Roman Empire during the Smalcaldic War, activity in Magdeburg rose.[64] Between 1548 and 1552, Magdeburg printers ran one-fourth of their entire sixteenth-century book production, earning the appellation "the chancery of God." In this flurry of polemical pamphlets, Lotter had the honor of printing the Magdeburg Confession.[65] Whereas other pamphlets during the Adiaphoristic Controversy were published in German, Lotter's press released both a German and Latin edition of the Magdeburg Confession, apparently seeking a larger audience, including those in legal and political roles beyond the German territories.[66]

The Restoration of Lutheran Saxony

Duke Maurice likely was not moved by the Magdeburg Confession nor even by the steadfast resolve of the Magdeburgers. He did, however, turn his thirteen-and-a-half-months' siege of Magdeburg (September 22, 1550–November 7, 1551)[67] into a victory for both Magdeburg and himself. After Flacius and Gallus published one last pamphlet in October 1551, this one on Acts 5:29, Maurice and the leaders of Magdeburg discussed conditions for concluding the siege: but it would be a "coming to terms" (*vertragen*), not "surrendering" (*ergeben*).[68] On November 9, Maurice entered the city, pronouncing amnesty to all. He went so far as to specifically name Flacius and Gallus in guarantee of their freedom.[69]

---

62 Kaufmann, "Our Lord God's Chancery," 573.

63 Olson, *Matthias Flacius*, 148.

64 Kaufmann, "Our Lord God's Chancery," 572.

65 Kaufmann, "Our Lord God's Chancery," 573. See also Rein, *Chancery of God*, 16–24.

66 Raley, "Martin Luther on the Legitimacy of Resisting the Emperor," 120. See below, "Recommended Reading," p. 26, for editions of the Magdeburg Confession.

67 Olson, *Matthias Flacius*, 168, 209.

68 Olson, *Matthias Flacius*, 211.

69 Olson, *Matthias Flacius*, 209–10.

Maurice's seemingly rapid change of course had been in preparation for months behind the scenes as he schemed against the emperor, who was carrying on his own plots against rivals in both Spain and France in an effort to secure a Holy Roman imperial dynasty.[70] In December 1550, Maurice had conducted diplomatic talks with leaders of the Königsberg Defense League, formed by Lutheran princes the preceding February. When the princes reorganized as the Torgau League in May 1551, Maurice was ready to promise support for Magdeburg, even as his siege against that city remained in place. In October 1551, Maurice conspired with King Henry II of France to attack Charles, an arrangement formalized by treaty on January 15, 1552. The siege of Magdeburg—and its real human costs on both sides of the lines—served to hide from the emperor the truth of Maurice's duplicity.[71] At the cost of Lutheran blood, Maurice bought himself time, drained the imperial treasury, and extended his own power.[72] Charles, "bankrupt and isolated," was slow to recognize Maurice's betrayal.[73]

The 1552 princes' revolt, as Maurice now sided with the Lutherans, succeeded where the Smalcaldic League had failed. Imperial forces were driven from Saxony, and papal mandates were ignored. Lutherans preached as Lutherans and administered the sacraments as Lutherans, without jumping through any interimistic hoops. John Frederick and Philip of Hesse were set free. Charles himself initially hoped the empire's concessions would be temporary, but within a few years, it became clear that he would be unable to return to the heights he had reached in 1547.[74] Unwilling to admit to a Lutheran victory in good conscience, Charles prepared to transfer the imperial crown to his brother, Ferdinand, who ultimately would concede.[75] Charles V's

70 Nexon, *Struggle for Power in Early Modern Europe*, 176. During this period, Charles V hoped that a general council of the church would make the Augsburg Interim permanent and thus solidify his position politically, But the Council of Trent, which initially held session from 1545 to 1547, would not reconvene until 1551. Meanwhile, the political and theological geography of the Holy Roman Empire kept fragmenting more quickly than Charles could piece it back together. See Martyn C. Rady, *The Emperor Charles V* (New York: Longman, 1998), 73–88.

71 Olson, *Matthias Flacius*, 211–13, here at p. 213.

72 Rady, *Emperor Charles V*, 85; Nexon, *Struggle for Power in Early Modern Europe*, 177 and 178 n. 162.

73 Parker, *Emperor*, 434–35.

74 Rady, *Emperor Charles V*, 86–87.

75 Parker, *Emperor*, 439.

dream of a united church under a Spanish throne crumbled, even as his own ill health left him scarcely capable of conducting his daily affairs.[76] The Peace of Passau of 1552—further solidified by the Peace of Augsburg of 1555—restricted imperial and papal interference in Saxony by stipulating that the local prince had authority to determine which religion would be practiced within his realm: "the triumph of principality over Empire, of prince over Emperor."[77] Under the principle *cujus regio ejus religio* (whose the region, his the religion),[78] Saxony would be Lutheran.[79] Maurice opportunistically presented himself as the protector of the churches of the Augsburg Confession in both Electoral and Ducal Saxony.

Ironically for the Lutherans, the pragmatic establishment of theological orthodoxy by a civil authority rendered an unorthodox result; moreover, this outcome was inevitable because the political process did not respect the Lutheran distinction between the two kingdoms. While the Magdeburg Confession preserved Lutheran orthodoxy against the compromising Philippists and the invading Romanists alike, Maurice's political victories at Passau and Augsburg subordinated Saxon churches under the Saxon states in what might be called a miniature Holy Lutheran Empire. But like the Holy Roman Empire, it was never as pure as it may have appeared on paper. The Peace of Augsburg was implemented unevenly at the local level, where a "web of negotiations" within a "bewildering context of traditional considerations" (kinship, social privilege, and political status, as well as theological confession) made it "possible for Lutheran officials to hold offices in a Catholic prince-bishopric" as decision-makers vacillated between pragmatism and indifference.[80] Meanwhile, the growing Calvinist presence in northern Europe would soon regard

76 Rady, *Emperor Charles V*, 92–93.

77 Alvarez, *Charles V*, 161. See also Whitford, *Tyranny and Resistance*, 90.

78 Coined in 1586 by Joachim Stephan, a law professor at the University of Greifswald, this dictum originally applied to the Peace of Augsburg (1555). It also describes a central tenet of the Peace of Westphalia (1648). See Peter H. Wilson, *Heart of Europe: A History of the Holy Roman Empire* (Cambridge, MA: The Belknap Press of Harvard University Press, 2016), 116, 127–28.

79 Nexon, *Struggle for Power in Early Modern Europe*, 176.

80 Richard J. Ninness, *Between Opposition and Collaboration: Nobles, Bishops, and the German Reformations in the Prince-Bishopric of Bamberg, 1555–1619* (Leiden: Brill, 2011), 203.

the Lutheran princes the way the Saxon pastors had once felt toward the emperor and the pope. Or, as in the case of the University of Marburg, a Calvinist ruler, Count Moritz of Hesse-Marburg, could in 1605 by *fiat* transform a Lutheran-founded institution into a university for his own confession. This action prompted Lutheran faculty to flee to the University of Giessen, which a rival count, Ludwig V of Hesse-Darmstadt, established in 1607 for Lutheranism. In 1624, an imperial court ruled that the University of Marburg should revert to Lutheranism on the basis of Ludwig IV's testament, shifting authority away from current leadership and toward prior legal claims.[81] This and sundry similar affairs illustrate how the seeds of the Thirty Years' War (1618–48) were planted within the uneasy soil of the Peace of Augsburg.[82] During the conflicts of the Thirty Years' War, Magdeburg would be sacked by the imperial army, injuring the German Lutheran pride that once had withstood pope, emperor, duke, and former Wittenberg mentors alike.[83] The siege of Magdeburg in 1631 was marked with an unusual scale of brutality, likened by contemporaries to Nebuchadnezzar's destruction of Jerusalem.[84] After much bloodshed, the Peace of Westphalia (1648) reinstated the Peace of Augsburg, while revising the normative year from 1555 to 1624: whoever controlled the region in that year, his the religion shall remain.[85]

Legacies of the Magdeburg Confession for German Lutheranism

The Magdeburg Confession reenacted Luther's stand at the Diet of Worms in a new context and for a new generation. By risking

81 The prevailing legal arguments were based in part on the distinction between person and office that resonated strongly with Luther's doctrine of vocation and was a pervasive theme within the Magdeburg Confession. Circumstantial and textual evidence both suggest that *Tractatus de regimine seculari et ecclesiastico* (1619), by German jurist Dietrich Reinking, relied also upon the Magdeburg Confession. See Paolo Astorri and Lars Cyril Nørsgaard, "Publicus—Privatus: The Divine Foundations of Authority in Dietrich Reinking," *Journal of Early Modern Christianity* 9, no. 1 (2022): 93–119, here at pp. 99–101, 114.

82 Cf. Nexon, *Struggle for Power in Early Modern Europe*, 182.

83 Kaufmann, "Our Lord God's Chancery," 569.

84 MacCulloch, *The Reformation*, 499.

85 Wilson, *Heart of Europe*, 116, 127–28.

martyrdom for the theology of the Augsburg Confession, Luther's successors became genuinely Lutheran, hence, "Gnesio-Lutheran." The old debate between Rome and Wittenberg soon was eclipsed by the debate that had emerged between the Gnesio-Lutherans and the Philippists, especially concerning adiaphora, in the aftermath of the Smalcaldic War. Ultimately, the Gnesio-Lutheran position prevailed. While Flacius had demanded a public confession of their interimistic errors, Melanchthon and Bugenhagen each privately confessed.[86] However, throughout the 1550s and 1560s, these two primary groups splintered into yet more factions,[87] even as Flacius experienced the satisfaction of the formal adoption of the Magdeburg Confession by a gathering of the Hanseatic Lutheran churches in 1557.[88]

In 1580, the publication of the Formula of Concord vindicated the Magdeburg position concerning adiaphora: "During a time of persecution, when a plain and steadfast confession is required of us, we should not yield to the enemies in such matters of adiaphora. . . . For in such a case it is no longer a question about adiaphora. But it concerns the truth of the Gospel" (Article X).[89] Removed, however, from the siege of Magdeburg by nearly three decades, the Formula left unaddressed the political implications of Flacius's theological dictum that nothing remains an adiaphoron when a clear confession is required to address a controversy: *"Nihil est adiaphoron in casu confessionis et scandali."*[90] It was, ultimately, more in keeping with the Peace of Augsburg's pragmatic statecraft than with the Magdeburg Confession's careful distinction between the two kingdoms[91] that Duke Frederick William (1562–1602) commissioned the Saxon Visitation Articles in 1592, which remained the state-imposed standard of Lutheran orthodoxy in Saxony until 1836.[92]

---

86 Olson, *Matthias Flacius*, 311.

87 Kolb, *Andreae and the Formula of Concord*, 26–42.

88 Olson, *Matthias Flacius*, 312.

89 FC Ep X 6 (*Concordia*, 497; cf. *BoC*, 516).

90 Olson, "Theology of Revolution," 68–69 (downplaying the political context); Olson, *Matthias Flacius*, 133 (the first appearance of Flacius's slogan in a pamphlet entitled *In These Strong Winds*).

91 See below, MC CA, pp. 74–81.

92 Cf. *Concordia*, 654.

Not only was Lutheranism preserved by the Magdeburg Confession and those who subscribed it, but Lutheran historiography was born in Magdeburg. In addition to his polemical writings, Flacius also was busy inventing the modern discipline of church history by collating records into the *Magdeburg Centuries*.[93] This ambitious feat of erudition for the first time organized the past not according to the lifespans of famous men but rather according to "centuries," from an old Latin word meaning "hundreds" that henceforth would have a new meaning, "hundred years." With attention shifting from persons to time itself, medieval hagiography would give way to modern objectivity,[94] even as the authority of pope and emperor alike had to give way to the order of God's three estates and the varied vocations within them. While the writings of Luther and Melanchthon had repeatedly treated the three estates, it was the succinct summary and timely application in the Magdeburg Confession that established as Lutheran orthodoxy a triple vocation for each person: *status ecclesiasticus, status politicus,* and *status oeconomicus*.[95]

This formulation, however, would soon be tested again. The Magdeburg Confession had justified political resistance by two estates which, within Magdeburg itself, acted harmoniously in 1550: the lesser magistrates within the civil order and the theologians within the ecclesiastical.[96] A decade later, a rift emerged between John Frederick the Middler of Ducal Saxony and certain Gnesio-Lutheran theologians whom he initially had sponsored during the establishment of the University of Jena. In 1561, a ducal order limited the preaching and publishing activities of four outspoken Jena theologians, requiring that their manuscripts be approved by the ducal court before publication. When the professors refused to be censored, they were dismissed from their posts and exiled. One of them, Matthaeus Judex, fled to Magdeburg, but there too a conflict emerged between the City Council and the theologians regarding who had authority to call pastors. Fleeing next to Wismar, Judex compiled the arguments that he and others had made in Jena into a book entitled *On the Invention*

93 Kaufmann, "Our Lord God's Chancery," 582.

94 Olson, *Matthias Flacius*, 257–63.

95 Luise Schorn-Schutte, "The Christian Clergy in the Early Modern Holy Roman Empire: A Comparative Social Study," *Sixteenth Century Journal* 29, no. 3 (1998): 717–31, here at p. 729.

96 See below, MC CA, pp. 74–81; MC Def, pp. 86–87; MC Exh, pp. 121–22.

of Printing and On the Legitimate Oversight of the Press.[97] Expanding upon the Magdeburg Confession, Judex insisted that a vocational distinction between leaders in the church and leaders in the state bars civil magistrates from encroaching upon the duty of theologians to publish God's truth.[98] While Judex articulated freedom of the press as an extension of Magdeburg theology, John Frederick the Middler insisted upon censorship as an extension of Saxon politics.

Legacies beyond the Lutheran Reformation

The adaptation of Magdeburg's distinctively Lutheran principles to the broader Protestant scene can be traced primarily to Theodore Beza's *Concerning the Rights of Rulers over Their Subjects and the Duty of Subjects toward Their Rulers* (1574), a work cleverly titled to avoid censorship. (Beza, writing anonymously, actually emphasized *duties* of rulers and *rights* of subjects.) His outline so closely tracked the Magdeburg Confession's arguments from Scripture, history, and positive law that some library catalogers regarded Beza's work as merely an updated edition of the Lutheran tract.[99] Beza, however, reshaped the argument in terms of a tripartite covenant between God, the rulers, and the ruled. In addition to this Calvinist emphasis on covenantal theology (which he predicated more on the New Testament theology of marriage than on the Old Testament covenant between God and Israel), he offered a more sophisticated political schematization, distinguishing between two classes of lesser magistrates: aristocrats and democratic representatives. Along the way, Beza elevated the rights of the people from being a consequence of good government to being a precondition for legitimate government.[100]

The Magdeburg Confession's influence also reached other prominent thinkers in England, Scotland, and British North America. A key link in the transmission of ideas was John Ponet, bishop of

97 Robert Kolb, "Matthaeus Judex's Condemnation of Princely Censorship of Theologians' Publications," *Church History* 50, no 4 (1981): 401–14, here at pp. 404–5.

98 Kolb, "Matthaeus Judex's Condemnation of Princely Censorship of Theologians' Publications," 412–13.

99 John Witte Jr., "Rights, Resistance, and Revolution in the Western Tradition: Early Protestant Foundations," *Law and History Review* 26, no. 3 (2008): 545–70, here at p. 556.

100 Witte, "Rights, Resistance, and Revolution," 555–70.

Rochester and Winchester, whose *Short Treatise on Political Power* (1556) brought Magdeburg's theology of resistance to England and, eventually, to the American colonies as well.[101] Just as Beza cited the Magdeburg Confession directly, so also did John Knox and Christopher Goodman, who were in conversation with each other and also had each read Ponet's treatise.[102] During the mid-1600s, the principles of the Magdeburg Confession became normative as Europe became modern; watershed events such as the Treaty of Westphalia (1648) and the English Civil War (1642–51) marked a turning point.[103] Soon direct citations of the Magdeburg Confession were eclipsed by new authors who adapted its principles to new contexts.

Consider, for example, the English poet John Milton, who today is best remembered for *Paradise Lost* (1667) but who also wrote theological tracts that fueled the English Revolution. He specifically defended both the overthrow and the execution of Charles I. Supporting the radical republicans, Milton published *The Tenure of Kings and Magistrates* (1649) just two weeks after the king's execution. The title page bore an extended subtitle that captured the core of Milton's convictions: "That it is Lawfull, and hath been held so through all Ages, for any, who have the Power, to call account a Tyrant, or wicked KING, and after due conviction, to depose, and put him to death; if the ordinary MAGISTRATE have neglected, or deny'd to doe it."[104] The Lesser Magistrate Doctrine that Milton promoted had its source in the Magdeburg Confession, which he referenced (likely having learned of it through Beza's work) in a commonplace notebook entry in the early 1640s.[105] Citing Romans 13 and 1 Peter 2, as

101 See the article by Whitford, above, p. 15 n. 57.

102 See Hildebrand, "The Magdeburg Bekenntnis as a Possible Link between German and English Resistance Theories," 227–53.

103 Symeon Mavridis, "The Revolution from Antiquity till 18th Century," *Sociology International Journal* 2, no. 5 (2018): 360–69, here at p. 366.

104 John Milton, *The Tenure of Kings and Magistrates* (1649), reprinted in *John Milton Prose: Major Writings on Liberty, Politics, Religion, and Education*, ed. David Loesenstein (Oxford: Wiley-Blackwell, 2013), 243–73; title page appears on p. 245.

105 See F. A. Patterson, ed., *The Works of John Milton*, 18 vols. (New York: Columbia University Press, 1931–38), 18:213, as cited by Martin Dzelzainis, "Milton and the Regicide," in *John Milton: Life, Writing, Reputation*, ed. Paul Hammond and Blair Worden (Oxford: Oxford University Press, 2010), 3 n. 6, accessed December 2021, www.researchgate.net. The deployment of the Magdeburg Confession by Milton specifically and Presbyterians generally is further discussed by Matthew Neufeld, "Doing

well as Revelation 13, Milton underscored in *Tenure* the two marks of legitimate human ordinance to be "the punishment of evildoers, and the encouragement of them that doe well." But "if the power be not such, or the person execute not such power, neither the one nor the other is of God, but of the Devil, and by consequence has to be resisted."[106] Like the signers of the Magdeburg Confession, Milton supported his claims by appeal to sacred history (especially from the period of ancient Israel's judges), secular history, and reason. Briefly mentioning the Smalcaldic War, but neglecting to reference the Magdeburg Confession directly, he devoted more attention to John Knox's revolt in Scotland.[107] "I doe not say it is rebellion, if the thing commanded though establish'd be unlawful, and that they sought first all due means of redress."[108] Like the Scottish Calvinists, Milton could endorse actions by the populace to overthrow an illegitimate regime and establish a new government in its place, which he considered "the necessary self-defence of a whole Common wealth."[109] More moderate than Knox or Milton in political philosophy, while devoutly uncompromising in theological confession, the Gnesio-Lutherans had sought not to overthrow but rather to preserve the lawful civil ordinances of Magdeburg, expressing a willingness to heed both magistrate and emperor provided neither overstepped the God-given limits of secular authority.[110]

Aside from Beza's heavy reliance on the Magdeburg Confession, which shaped Milton's defense of the English Revolution, scholars have asserted an indirect, mediated influence of the Magdeburg

without Precedent: Applied Typology and the Execution of Charles I in Milton's 'Tenure of Kings and Magistrates,'" *Sixteenth Century Journal*, 38, no. 2 (2007): 329–44, here at p. 330.

106 Milton, *Tenure of Kings and Magistrates*, 253.

107 Milton, *Tenure of Kings and Magistrates*, 258–60. Concerning Knox's appropriation of the Magdeburg principles, see Steven Ozment, *The Age of Reform: 1250–1550, An Intellectual and Religious History of Late Medieval and Reformation Europe* (New Haven: Yale University Press, 1981), ch. 14, especially pp. 419–22.

108 Milton, *Tenure of Kings and Magistrates*, 260.

109 Milton, *Tenure of Kings and Magistrates*, 271.

110 For a more recent Christian Restorationist appropriation of the Magdeburg Confession as a stepping stone toward Knox's bolder development of the doctrine of the lesser magistrate, see Matthew J. Trewhella, *The Doctrine of the Lesser Magistrates: A Proper Resistance to Tyranny and a Repudiation of Unlimited Obedience to Civil Government* (CreateSpace, 2013).

Confession on a number of important contributors to modern Western civilization, including John Adams in the eighteenth century as well as Dietrich Bonhoeffer and Norwegian bishop Eivind Berggrav in the twentieth century.[111] These investigations suggest that the historical impact of the Magdeburg Confession has been dramatically underestimated and provide more than adequate justification for this new English edition.

Epilogue

Why did Stephanus Tucher desire so strongly for his name to be recorded on the Magdeburg Confession? Why did the others, who by living would have to endure a year-long siege of their city and their churches, also sign? The historical context outlined above suggests answers to questions of motivation. Other, more enduring questions stretch beyond the lives of the Magdeburg Confession's signers. Where, exactly, is the line between ecclesiastical and civil authority to be drawn? What is the remedy when someone crosses that line in either direction? Who is responsible for implementing that remedy? In addressing these perennial concerns, the Magdeburg Confession remains a fruitful document for contemporary discussions of political resistance, church-state relations, and the doctrine of vocation.

111 Robert Kolb, "Magdeburg as a Bridge: From Reformation to Orthodoxy," *Proslogion: Studies in Medieval and Early Modern Social History and Culture* 6, no. 2 (2022): 238–60; Whitford, "John Adams, John Ponet, and a Lutheran Influence on the American Revolution"; Michael P. DeJonge, *Bonhoeffer's Reception of Luther* (Oxford: Oxford University Press, 2017), especially 68–75, 83–85, 196–203; Michael P. DeJonge, *Bonhoeffer on Resistance: The Word against the Wheel* (Oxford: Oxford University Press, 2018), 39–40; Eric Metaxas, *Bonhoeffer: Pastor, Martyr, Prophet, Spy* (Nashville: Thomas Nelson, 2010), 150–56; Richard A. Loomis, "Dietrich Bonhoeffer's Journey of Resistance," in *History (1933–1948): What We Choose to Remember*, ed. Margaret Monahan Hogan and James M. Lies (Portland: University of Portland, 2011), 135–48; Whitford, *Tyranny and Resistance*, 102–4, 118 n. 21; Peter Lampe, "Widerstand bei Luther: Vortrag auf dem Rittertag der Pommerschen Genossenschaft in Worms 2017," *Der Greif* 1 (2018): 26–33, here at pp. 31–32; John Witte Jr. "'We Must Obey God Rather Than Men': Lutheran Resistance against Pope and Emperor in the Reformation Era," in *Uncivil Disobedience: Theological Perspectives*, ed. David Gides (Minneapolis: Lexington Books, 2023), 75–92; Ryan C. MacPherson, "Political Resistance in Lutheran Theology: The Lawful Authority of Romans 13 versus the Two Beasts of Revelation 13," in *My Savior's Guest: A Festschrift in Honor of Erling Trygve Teigen*, ed. Thomas Rank (Lake Mills, IA: Thomas Rank, 2021), 127–47. For more on Berggrav, see below, p. 29 n. 7.

Recommended Reading

Editions of the Magdeburg Confession

Bekentnis [Bekenntnis] Vnterricht und vermanung, der Pfarrhern und Prediger, der Christlichen Kirchen zu Magdeburk anno 1550. den 13. Aprilis. Magdeburg: M. Lotther, 1550.

Reprinted in Friederich Hortleder. *Von Rechtmässigkeit Anfang Fort-und endlichen Außgang deß Teutschen Kriegs Keyser Carls deß Fünfften wider die Schmalkaldische Bundsoberste.* Gotha: W. Endter, 1645. 2:1053–91. http://resolver.staatsbibliothek-berlin.de/SBB00027F3200010000.

Reprinted in Hans-Joachim Köhler, comp. *Flugschriften des späteren 16. Jahrhunderts.* Leiden: IDC, 1990–. FF. 185–6#567.Hor

Digitized archive: *Controversia et Confessio Digital.* Herausgegeben von Irene Dingel. https://www.controversia-et-confessio.de/id/c832b333-9dbe-4b9a-92b0-1abc0eb8e698.

Reprinted as "Magdeburger Bekenntnis (1550)," in *Der Adiaphoristische Streit* (1548–1560). *Controversia et Confessio* 2. Edited by Irene Dingel. Göttingen: Vanderhoeck & Ruprecht, 2012. Pages 458–629.

Confessio et apologia pastorum & reliquorum ministrorum ecclesiæ Magdeburgensis, anno 1550. idibus Aprilis. Magdeburg: Lotter, 1550.

Digitized archive: https://www.google.com/books/edition/_/fIFUAAAAcAAJ?hl=en&gbpv=1.

The Magdeburg Confession, 13th of April 1550 A.D. Translated by Matthew Colvin. North Charleston, SC: CreateSpace, 2012.

Interpretations of the Magdeburg Confession

Kaufmann, Thomas. *Das Ende der Reformation: Magdeburgs "Herrgotts Kanzlei" (1548–1551/2).* Tübingen: Mohr Siebeck, 2003. An analysis of the pamphlets from the Adiaphoristic Controversy, the chief conclusions of which are also available in English: Thomas Kaufmann, "'Our Lord God's Chancery' in Magdeburg and Its Fight against the Interim," *Church History* 73, no. 3 (2004): 566–82.

Olson, Oliver K. *Matthias Flacius and the Survival of Luther's Reform.* Wiesbaden: Harrassowitz, 2002. A sympathetic account, situating the Magdeburg Confession within the life of the leader of the Gnesio-Lutheran party.

Rein, Nathan. *The Chancery of God: Protestant Print, Polemic and Propaganda against the Empire, Magdeburg, 1546–1551.* Hampshire: Ashgate, 2008. A critical interpretation, analyzing the Magdeburg Confession in the context of pamphlets that shaped, and in some degree were shaped by, the popular culture's fusion of politics, theology, and ethnicity.

Whitford, David Mark. *Tyranny and Resistance: The Magdeburg Confession and the Lutheran Tradition.* St. Louis: Concordia Publishing House, 2001. An accessible account spanning the Peasants' War to the Peace of Augsburg.

COMMENTARY ON THE MAGDEBURG CONFESSION

THE Magdeburg Confession marshals arguments from Holy Scripture and the Augsburg Confession to establish a proper understanding of the church and her ministry. The confession draws from both Holy Scripture and natural law to establish a proper understanding of secular authority in relation to the Christian Church and the Christian home. From history—both secular and sacred—the confessors further illustrate the proper relationship between church and state, much as Aristotle, in his *Politics*, draws inductions from patterns observed in various city-states. Schooled in the late-medieval art of disputation, the confessors arrange their points with clear logic while pointing out the fallacious reasoning of their opponents. Above all, they write with pastoral concern for the souls within Magdeburg, whom they are shielding from imperial attack, and for the souls beyond Magdeburg, who lately had succumbed to the papacy's "deceits."[1] While the confession necessarily deals with political matters and recent historical developments, the focus never departs from the spiritual salvation achieved for sinners by Christ or the ministry and the means of grace by which His eternal benefits come to those who place their faith in Him.

Syllogism (MC Syl)

Just as Luther's Small Catechism concisely previews his Large Catechism, just as the Augsburg Confession is a quicker read than the Apology of the Augsburg Confession, just as the Formula of Concord consists of both a concise Epitome and an expansive Solid Declaration, so also the Magdeburg Confession begins with a "Syllogism Summarizing the Argument of This Book." Here the seed

---

1 See the historical introduction above, p. 3; and below, MC Post, p. 125.

of orthodoxy becomes firmly planted in the reader's mind, where its roots may deepen and its fruits may appear when the full confession is read in the pages that follow. The title "Syllogism" (*Syllogismus*) however, suggests that something more than a preview is being provided here. Indeed, the next section is called the "Preface" (*Praefatio*), and it summarizes the Adiaphoristic Controversy, identifies the vocations proper to church and to state, and underscores the importance of believing, confessing, and defending the Christian faith—whether against foes within the church or in the state or both.[2] Why, then, also include a "syllogism"?

Syllogismus can refer to deductive reasoning in general, but it especially refers to a form of logical argument consisting of three propositions: the major premise, the minor premise, and the conclusion. Aristotle developed a detailed account explaining which kinds of syllogisms were valid and which were invalid and why they each were so. Six of Aristotle's works on logic became collectively known as the *Organon* (or "Tool"), and these were fundamental to medieval education and repurposed at the University of Wittenberg for the Lutheran cause.[3] In Melanchthon's confessional writings (the Augsburg Confession and its Apology), as well as his *Commentary on Romans*, the analysis of syllogisms carries much weight in establishing theological truth.[4] Provided that terms are clearly defined (by avoiding ambiguity or equivocation), that the two premises are in fact true (that is, revealed by God to man by Scripture or by natural law or by both), and that the premises logically entail the conclusion (as set forth in Aristotle's rules of reasoning), then a syllogism is sound, which is to say, there is no rational basis for rejecting the conclusion. Every man of sane mind must accept the conclusion.[5]

---

2 See below, MC Pref, pp. 45–51.

3 Nicole Kuropka, "Philip Melanchthon and Aristotle," in *Philip Melanchthon: Theologian in Classroom, Confession, and Controversy*, ed. Herman J. Selderhuis (Göttingen: Vandenhoeck & Ruprecht, 2012), 19–28.

4 For example, Ap II 51; III 79, 237; VI 26; XXIV 87; XIX 89; Philip Melanchthon, *Commentary on Romans*, trans. Fred Kramer (St. Louis: Concordia Publishing House, 1992), *passim*.

5 For a clear and concise presentation of Aristotle's principles of logic, which the faculty at Wittenberg also taught, see "All of Logic in Two Pages," in Peter Kreeft, *Socratic Logic*, ed. Trent Dougherty, ed. 3.1 (South Bend, IN: St. Augustine's Press, 2010), 26–27.

To call the introductory section of the Magdeburg Confession a "Syllogism" is, then, to accuse any who reject the confession not merely of religio-political factionalism but also of irrationality. A logician's tone continues throughout the work: "any sane observer will be quick to understand"; "every sane person now understands this"; "when tyrants rise to such insanity"; "no sane person would deny it"; "I leave it to any pious and sane person to contemplate"; and, most explicitly, "Unless perhaps, when it comes to the argument for a lawful defense, the will of the king and his weapons have changed the very concepts of divine and natural law, cause and effect, and all the rules of logic, as they have been able to do in many articles of Christian teaching up to this point."[6] To abandon reason is to embrace Machiavellian absolutism:[7] in that case, "the truth of knowledge and the law of cause and effect will always depend on the whim and arms of those who have more power."[8]

In the Lutheran mind, faith often exceeds reason, but reason does not, strictly speaking, contradict faith; rather, reason can be deployed to support those aspects of an article of faith that are within reason's reach. Luther's memorable rants against reason—a whore, a witch, and so forth—were, read in context, criticisms not of reason itself but of the abuses of right reason that characterized the false theologies of Zwingli and others.[9] Luther himself often reasoned syllogistically, as in his *Heidelberg Disputation* (1518) and his *Disputation concerning the Passage: "The Word Was Made Flesh"* (1539).[10]

The deployment of a syllogism to introduce the Magdeburg Confession furthermore brings to mind the style of education

6 See below, MC Def, pp. 86, 92, 96, 97, 98, 88.

7 Machiavelli and Luther were contemporaries. The debate surrounding the Magdeburg Confession was shaped by popular convictions that one could not be both a faithful Christian and a Machiavellian pragmatist (see Rein, *Chancery of God*, 197, 212). Bishop Eivind Berggrav of Oslo, who led the Norwegian Lutheran resistance movement against Nazism (see the historical introduction above, p. 25), instructively compared Machiavelli's and Luther's views regarding proper limits of secular power. See Eivind Berggrav, *Man and State*, trans. George Aus (Philadelphia: Muhlenberg Press, 1951), 5–12.

8 See below, MC Def, p. 88.

9 For example, see Luther, *Confession concerning Christ's Supper* (1528), especially AE 37:179–80, 195, 201–12. See also Jerry K. Robbins, "Luther and Reason: A Reappraisal," *Word and World* 13, no. 2 (1993): 191–202.

10 AE 31:39–58; 38:239–77.

developed by Luther and Melanchthon at the University of Wittenberg. Melanchthon promoted neo-Aristotelianism at Wittenberg, against both the shoddy scholasticism of the Papists and the irreverent irrationalism of the Anabaptists. The Wittenberg faculty, including Melanchthon's star pupil Matthias Flacius, modeled the art of disputation for their students. Candidates for the master's diploma in turn had to perform a disputation of their own. Those disputations included syllogistic arguments, with close evaluation of the premises and their logical connections to the conclusion, always defining terms carefully and in accordance with Holy Scripture.[11]

Under duress, however, Melanchthon's pragmatic aim to preserve his university clouded his otherwise logically clear and biblically faithful intellect. By making his peace with the Augsburg Interim, Melanchthon would keep Wittenberg open. Flacius felt betrayed and fled to Magdeburg, where his preaching and writing fomented the courage that would lead local clergy to affix their names to the Magdeburg Confession.

Articulated by Lutheran logicians who, like Flacius, preserved Melanchthon's methods but did not share his conclusions when it came to the Adiaphoristic Controversy, the Magdeburg Confession boils down to this:

1. A lesser magistrate is duty-bound by God to resist a higher magistrate who violently persecutes God's people.
2. The emperor is a higher magistrate who is violently persecuting God's people.
3. Therefore, the magistrates of Magdeburg are duty-bound by God to resist the emperor.[12]

---

11 James Atkinson, "Luther and the Wittenberg Disputations, 1535–36," *Tyndale Bulletin* 33, no. 1 (1982): 31–57; Ernest G. Schwiebert, "The Reformation and Theological Education at Wittenberg," *Springfielder* 28, no. 3 (1964): 9–43. See also AE 72–73, which present (in addition to those already translated in previous volumes of the American edition) the disputations over which Luther presided or for which he wrote theses. An extensive introduction to the disputation process and its use at the university and as a means to present Luther's theology can be found in AE 72.

12 See below, MC Syl, p. 43.

Premise 1 (the major premise) is established by arguments from Scripture in the confession's "On Defense."[13] Premise 2 (the minor premise) is established, first, by identifying the Lutherans as God's people by virtue of the Augsburg Confession, itself identified as orthodox, biblical doctrine in the Chief Articles of the Magdeburg Confession;[14] and, second, by appeal to broadly disseminated knowledge that the emperor is indeed persecuting the Lutherans.[15] Finally, in the confession's "Exhortation," the implications of the syllogism are drawn out, encouraging the faithful to perform their duties of resisting the emperor's persecution "according to their calling."[16]

Preface (MC Pref)

According to the Augsburg Interim, each Lutheran church was required to suspend the Augsburg Confession until such time as "a future synod" renders a final decision. The Magdeburg Confession clarifies that such a synod would be under the auspices of "her [the Lutheran churches'] known enemy and persecutor." Thus this promise to abide by the Council of Trent in the name of "adiaphora" constitutes a "real rejection of the entire Augsburg Confession and with it also a rejection of Christ Himself."[17] Whether lesser magistrates may take steps to defend the local populace against imperial tyranny would be addressed shortly. First, it is to be noted that "it belongs to our office" as pastors to "publicly set forth something for the purpose of vindicating in some way the revealed doctrine of the Gospel against this unjust oppression."[18] In other words, Lutherans are confessors. Pastors speak with a prophetic voice not merely to their flock—their local congregation—but also to the broader world.

13 See below, MC Def, pp. 85–108.

14 See below, MC CA, pp. 53–84.

15 See below, MC Syl, p. 43–44.

16 See below, MC Syl, p. 44; cf. MC Exh, pp. 109–24.

17 See below, MC Pref, pp. 48, 49.

18 See below, MC Pref, p. 49.

Chief Articles of the Lutheran Faith (MC CA)

Readers who today seek within the Magdeburg Confession a justification for popular political revolt will be tempted to skip the longest section, the Chief Articles. Here the Magdeburg Lutherans summarized and reaffirmed the Augsburg Confession, laying special emphasis on the Gospel, the office of the ministry, and the means of grace. At first glance, these topics have nothing to do with developing a theory of political resistance against tyranny. Upon closer inspection, however, they have everything to do with the Magdeburgers' resolve to withstand an imperial siege for more than a year. The office of preaching and administering the sacraments belongs to the church and is to be exercised by its properly called pastors. The state should not interfere. Nor should ecclesiastical authorities modify what Christ Himself instituted and what Christ Himself gave to His church.

The confession therefore presents the doctrines of the Holy Trinity, creation, the Law, the Gospel and justification, the sacraments, the church and her ministers, and the government and the household. These sections track closely with the Augsburg Confession but also include points of emphasis specific to the events occurring in Magdeburg in 1550.

The discussion of creation, for example, emphasized also the fall into sin, which both explains the ubiquity of human vice in society and also disproves the papal teaching that enough good remained in man to "either satisfy the Law of God or merit grace by congruent merit."[19]

The article concerning God's moral law identified the Ten Commandments and natural law as God's two means of revealing His plan for civil order. Furthermore, it criticized the Anabaptists for their anarchy and the Papists for their institution of new ordinances in the place of God's commands.[20] The two erring Lutheran camps, the Interimists and the Adiaphorists, were not quite so bad as the Papists, who "teach the godless doctrine that the Law was given for justification,"[21] but nonetheless those erring Lutherans "are restoring

19 See below, MC CA, p. 56.

20 See below, MC CA, pp. 58–60.

21 See below, MC CA, p. 59.

these very works of human tradition . . . [and] confirming the authority by which these godless opinions arose."[22]

The longest article focuses upon the Gospel and justification, presenting a Lutheran account of forensic justification whereby sinners are declared forgiven for Christ's sake and Christ's righteousness is imputed to them by faith as they are adopted into God's family and receive newness of life.[23] This article specifically rejects the errors of the Interimists, who "understand faith . . . only as the knowledge of the history concerning Christ" and not as "the fullness and confidence of trust in Christ."[24] The Adiaphorists, meanwhile, confuse civic righteousness (which a person can to some extent achieve through natural abilities that remain after the fall into sin) with righteousness before God (which no man can achieve or even contribute toward, but Christ alone possesses by His own virtue and imputes graciously to those who believe in Him).[25] While both the Interimists and Adiaphorists claim the mantle of the Augsburg Confession, the Magdeburg Confession insists that their "sophistries," borrowed from the church's "adversaries," cannot "prevent the godless opinions themselves from entering in."[26]

The Interimists bear guilt equal to that of the Papists when it comes to adulterations of the Lord's Supper. The Papists insisted that the laity should receive only Christ's body, not His blood; the Interimists were "offering both kinds of the Sacrament to the laity for a time, not because of Christ's institution but by their own special permission." Moreover, they, like the Papists, "ignore faith" and "attribute the reception of Christ's benefits" in the Sacrament "to the sacrifice that happens in the Mass."[27] The Adiaphorists, similarly, were "reinstituting the Papist Mass" and "opening an obvious door for reinstituting all the papistic abominations."[28]

Membership in the true church is not a matter of public allegiance to the papacy, but rather it is an invisible matter of faith in the heart,

22 See below, MC CA, pp. 58–59.

23 See below, MC CA, pp. 60–61.

24 See below, MC CA, p. 65.

25 See below, MC CA, p. 66.

26 See below, MC CA, pp. 66–67.

27 See below, MC CA, p. 71.

28 See below, MC CA, p. 72.

which may be recognized outwardly only by the divinely established marks of the church: "the ministry of the Word and Sacraments, sometimes pure and sometimes less pure. By this ministry the whole church becomes visible, though in it there are very many evil men."[29] This ministry belongs to all believers and is exercised by the men who receive a call among them to serve as pastors.[30] Christ has established the church to be governed by His Word, so that no one has authority to claim a unique title of "vicar of Christ."[31] "Instead of being the vicar of Christ, he [the pope] has truly become the vicar of the devil and the Antichrist."[32] "The Adiaphorists greatly aid these horrible abominations when they hand over the honor of primacy to the pope."[33]

Finally, God has established vocations so that people "serve one another" and "harmonize one with the other" as a father serves his children and a magistrate serves his community.[34] The magistrate must be "lawfully called" and, in accordance with Romans 13, "defend pious and honest citizens and subjects, and the church in particular, against the violence of evil men."[35] However, "when magistrates or parents lead those under them from piety and honesty, no obedience is owed them as if God commanded it. . . . Instead of an institution of God they become an institution of the devil, which can and ought to be resisted according to one's vocation."[36]

In summarizing Holy Scripture and drawing upon the heritage of the Augsburg Confession, the Magdeburg Confession seeks to avoid introducing anything novel or divisive into the church, but rather to confess with the church catholic that which ought to be universally accepted. "Therefore, we have now written this confession in our

29 See below, MC CA, pp. 74–75.

30 See below, MC CA, p. 75.

31 The bull of Pope Boniface VIII (r. 1294–1303), *Unam sanctam* (1302), asserted that the pope is the vicar of Christ and that all authority, temporal and spiritual, has been entrusted to him. See Denzinger, nos. 468–469.

32 See below, MC CA, pp. 77–78.

33 See below, MC CA, p. 78.

34 See below, MC CA, p. 79.

35 See below, MC CA, p. 79.

36 See below, MC CA, p. 80.

name and the name of our churches and in the name of all outside our walls who are still pious, who have not yet bowed the knee to Baal."[37]

On Defense (MC Def)

The confession, having established its orthodox Lutheran foundation, proceeds next to establish and apply a doctrine of political resistance. Nowhere, however, is their any hint of rebellion. Far from overthrowing secular authority, the confessors rely upon lawful civil ordinances. They plead that their "case be heard in a legitimate court."[38] They insist that they "are still right to demand" their right."[39] They work with and through the City Council of Magdeburg, which "is simply unwilling to reject the true doctrine and right forms of worship and to receive again false teachings, idolatries, and blasphemies."[40] Provided that orthodox Lutheranism may be practiced, "our City Council and our citizens will be most obedient to your Majesty [Charles V], in all their proper duties and according to the laws."[41] This strategy of honoring God's established positions of authority while also critiquing officeholders who speciously claim Romans 13 in favor of their own tyranny of course raises the question of "whether a Christian magistrate can or ought to protect his lands, and the Christian teachers and hearers in them, against his higher magistrate, and to repel him by force if he attempts to violently compel his lands into a rejection of the true teaching and right worship of God and into the acceptance of idolatry instead."[42] The Magdeburg Confession answers the question in the affirmative, on the basis of three arguments.

The First Argument (MC Def)

From "the clear Word of God, from absolutely unchangeable natural principles, and from the witness of the events themselves,"[43] the Magdeburg Confession concluded that among various magistrates

37 See below, MC CA, p. 84.

38 See below, MC Def, p. 86.

39 See below, MC Def, p. 86.

40 See below, MC Def, p. 87.

41 See below, MC Def, p. 90.

42 See below, MC Def, p. 87.

43 See below, MC Def, p. 98.

"each individually ought to persevere in performing the office of magistrate according to his station and in what way he can." A lesser magistrate who does nothing to check a tyrant from the top "commit[s] a great crime by this negligence."[44] That being said, not all injustices are equal. "Different levels of crimes or injustices" require proportionate responses by those who have vocations to respond.[45] The confession enumerates four specific levels of injustice, building upon Gregor Brück's (ca. 1485–1557) theory of *notoria injuria* that had won the consensus at Torgau twenty years earlier.[46]

1. "Not overly severe or irremediable": When a ruler, as result of natural weakness, falls into the occasional vice of misusing his office, the people should quietly bear in patience while lesser magistrates may intervene by reminding the ruler of the proper limits of his office.[47]
2. "Severe and wicked injustices": When a ruler more systematically acts "against oath and laws," then "no one who himself also holds a magistracy should be terrified by God's command from using his right as a magistrate to put up a necessary defense" on behalf of the people. Even so, Christian charity calls upon both the people and their lesser magistrates to consider bearing patiently, "if the injustice extends only to them or only to a few and can be tolerated without sin."[48]
3. When "forced to obvious sin": When a lesser magistrate cannot comply with the dictates of the higher magistrate except by committing a sin against God, then the lesser magistrate not only may but indeed now must resist. However, one should not rashly conclude that the injustice

44 See below, MC Def, pp. 94–95.

45 See below, MC Def, p. 95.

46 David M. Whitford, "From Speyer to Magdeburg: The Development and Maturation of a Hybrid Theory of Resistance to Tyranny," *Archive for Reformation History* 96, no. 1 (2005): 57–80, here at p. 65. See also the historical introduction above, pp. 7–8. The following enumeration and explanation is adapted from Ryan C. MacPherson, "Lutheran Theology and Political Resistance," presented at the Ottawa Circuit Online Conference, October 5–6, 2020.

47 See below, MC Def, p. 95.

48 See below, MC Def, pp. 95–96.

has progressed from the second level to the third. One must instead seek "careful and true wisdom, so that no higher laws are violated in warding off the injustice." Otherwise, premature resistance would weaken rather than restore God's established secular order.[49] When an injustice of the third level occurs, the ruler rightly should be called a "tyrant."[50]

4. "More than tyrannical": When a ruler persecutes not merely persons here and there, but systematically persecutes "their right itself," and thereby "persecute[s] God as the Author of this right," then the ruler has become (now citing Luther) a "bear-wolf" and "the very devil himself."[51] At this point, such an antichrist "must be resisted by everyone, even by the lowest and weakest magistrates, with all the power they possess."[52]

The Second Argument (MC Def)

Christ's command to "render to Caesar the things that are Caesar's, and to God the things that are God's" in Matthew 22:21 must be understood in light of Peter's dictum in Acts 5:29 that "we must obey God rather than men." Indeed, the Matthew passage itself shows that "Christ does not want what belongs to God attributed to Caesar, neither does He want what belongs to others attributed to Caesar, when they simply are not his according to either divine or even imperial law."[53]

Here the Magdeburg Confession follows not merely the Lutheran theology of vocation but also a broadly Western legal tradition in which person and office must be distinguished.[54] Just because a person who holds an office commands something does not mean obedience is owed, unless the command is within the scope of that

49 See below, MC Def, p. 96.

50 See below, MC Def, p. 96.

51 See below, MC Def, p. 96.

52 See below, MC Def, p. 97.

53 See below, MC Def, p. 100.

54 For example, Cicero's *De officiis* (Concerning Duties) was appropriated into Lutheran education by Melanchthon at Wittenberg. Schwiebert, "Reformation and Theological Education at Wittenberg," 25.

office. A husband and father, for example, who comes home in order to prostitute his wife and daughters to wicked men is himself wickedly violating his office within the family. The wife and daughters who ordinarily would owe him respect and obedience are under no such obligation in these grotesque circumstances; indeed, "they should also drive him back with stones, since they cannot otherwise preserve their chastity."[55]

That which is "outside of and contrary to his office" has become "the ordinance of the devil," no longer the "ordinance of God" in Romans 13.[56] To such tyrants, God Himself proclaims that "I will have no regard for your majesty and your authority" but indeed will raise up another with authority, "according to his vocation," to punish the tyrant.[57]

The Third Argument (MC Def)

The logical technique known as "reduction to absurdity" further supports the conclusion that those who wield power are not entitled to absolute obedience. If God really had commanded absolute obedience, then "it would follow that God, by His own ordinance and command, was fortifying, no, more than that, was honoring and helping evil, and that He was impeding the good, no, more than that, destroying the good!"[58] To follow the pope's demands is to support not Christ, but the Antichrist.[59]

Conversely, "when a magistrate restrains a tyrant, it is clear that the same tyrant has been restrained by God."[60] Here again, the obvious assumption is that "lawful civil ordinances" (AC XVI 1) may be recognized by the divinely established marks of secular justice: the punishment of evildoers and the protection of the innocent. A tyrant abandons these marks, but a Jehu, a Maccabee, an Asa, or an Ambrose who keeps a tyrant in check thereby restores the marks of secular justice.[61] Such "events recorded in biblical, ecclesiastical, and pagan history"

55 See below, MC Def, p. 100.

56 See below, MC Def, p. 101.

57 See below, MC Def, p. 102, paraphrasing Psalm 82:6.

58 See below, MC Def, p. 102.

59 See below, MC Def, p. 103.

60 See below, MC Def, p. 104.

61 See below, MC Def, pp. 106–7.

demonstrate the divinely established vocations of "lower magistrates putting up a defense against higher magistrates."[62] The "sanctuary of natural law itself" vindicates Emperor Trajan, who commanded his troops to render unto Caesar only that which actually is Caesar's: "Use this sword against my enemies if I command what is just. But if I command what is unjust, use it against me."[63]

A Theological Exhortation to Political Resistance (MC Exh)

The Magdeburg Confession concludes with an epilogue that reiterates the sincerely uttered and demonstrably established charge that the Augsburg Interim is the work of the Antichrist. The response of the faithful now must be obvious. "No godly or Christian man can aid our enemies."[64] To do so is to commit spiritual treason, for which ignorance is no excuse.[65] The enemies of the Augsburg Confession have "depart[ed] from the Word" and committed a "sin against the Holy Spirit."[66] Christians are called to "fight for the Gospel of Jesus Christ against Satan and his ministers, not only by refuting his lies but also by impeding his slaughters, since it is by both of these tactics that he is now so violently assaulting the true religion."[67]

The church as a whole begins with prayer to God on behalf of one another, continues with supplications to magistrates to fulfill their God-given offices, and culminates, when the necessity of an injustice of the third or fourth level fosters the duty, to "do for the protection of Christ the very things the enemies are insisting on doing for the destruction of Christ."[68] While it remains true of Christians collectively that they must wield both the Word and the sword, it does not follow that this applies to each Christian individually in the same way. Rather, God calls upon teachers to teach, magistrates to wield the sword, and subjects to obey their magistrates whenever their

62 See below, MC Def, p. 106.

63 See below, MC Def, pp. 107–8.

64 See below, MC Exh, p. 109.

65 See below, MC Exh, p. 110.

66 See below, MC Exh, pp. 111, 112.

67 See below, MC Exh, p. 114.

68 See below, MC Exh, p. 120.

commands are godly—"each one according to his place and station in life, without confusion."[69]

Vocation receives repeated emphasis, a pattern peculiar to Lutherans: "each one in his own place."[70] The Magdeburg Confession does not conclude by calling people to arms, but rather by arming people with their vocations and calling them to trust that God remains at work in, with, and under the offices of pastor and parishioner; emperor, magistrate, and subject; father, mother, and child. It was, after all, the singing of parents and children that first brought the pure Gospel to the churches of Magdeburg, and it was the pastors of Magdeburg's Lutheran churches who had instructed the civil magistrates in their proper duties to God and to man.

While later radicals would seek within the Magdeburg Confession or its derivative treatises a justification for political revolt, the Lutheran pastors had an aim both more sober and more supernal: "May our heavenly Father so govern the outcome of these dangerous events to the benefit of us all, so that the Antichrist cannot triumph with his father, the devil."[71] Maintaining a clear distinction between the two kingdoms, they did not imagine an immediately visible victory but resolved in Christ's name to "be glorified with Him, as we also suffer with Him and are killed for His sake all the day."[72]

69 See below, MC Exh, p. 122.

70 See below, MC Exh, p. 123; cf. MC CA, p. 79; MC Def, pp. 95, 103, 104.

71 See below, MC Exh, p. 123.

72 See below, MC Exh, p. 123, a paraphrase conjoining Romans 8:17 and Psalm 44:22.

Confession and Apology

OF THE PASTORS AND OTHER MINISTERS OF THE CHURCH OF MAGDEBURG

April 13, 1550

Psalm [119:46]
"I spoke of Your testimonies before kings,
and I was not put to shame."

Romans 13[:3]
"Princes are not a terror to the good work,
but to the evil."

Acts 9[:5]
"Saul, Saul, why are you persecuting Me?
It is hard for you to kick against the goads."

SYLLOGISM SUMMARIZING THE ARGUMENT OF THIS BOOK

WHEN the higher magistrate is violently persecuting the law itself among his subjects, whether natural law or divine, or the true religion and worship of God,[1] then the lesser magistrate ought to resist him, and this according to God's command.

The persecution which is now inflicted on us by higher magistrates is especially directed at the oppression of our true religion, the true worship of God, etc.[2]

Therefore, our magistrate ought to resist this oppression, and this according to God's command.

We prove the major premise of this syllogism by sure arguments from the Word of God in the second part of our little book.[3]

There are two parts to the minor premise. First, that the churches of this city have the true religion and true worship practices.[4] To this pertains the confession of our and our churches' doctrine and faith according to the articles of the Augsburg Confession, which is contained in the first part of this little book.[5] The second part of the minor premise is that the persecution we are suffering is aimed directly at the oppression of the true religion, etc. In this matter, the consciences of all men agree with us, and the very circumstance speaks for itself

1 The German version has *Gottesdienst* for the Latin *cultus Dei* here and throughout the entire Confession, signifying especially church services.

2 The German adds: "and the reintroduction of the pope's lies and horrible idolatry," as often elsewhere.

3 See below, MC Def, pp. 85–108.

4 Latin: *veros cultus*

5 See below, MC CA, pp. 53–84.

that this is being done. Our City Council has shown this in its own writings, and we demonstrate it repeatedly in this, our writing.[6]

From this syllogism, finally, come the very serious grounds for the exhortation that we make in the third part of this little book.[7] There we warn the faithful not to aid the enemy against us or altogether refuse their help to us. There we also encourage the faithful not to lose heart as they suffer and, according to their calling, to fight off this persecution of the Gospel and of Christ.

6 The City Council of Magdeburg issued no fewer than five decrees to this effect from 1548 through 1550 (*AS* 459 n. 10).

7 See below, MC Exh, pp. 109–23.

PREFACE

IN His immense kindness, God raised up Dr. Martin Luther, a veritable third Elijah,[1] that he might reveal in these last days, according to the prophecies proclaimed in Scripture, the man of sin, the son of perdition, the Antichrist, the Roman pope reigning in the temple of God, in order to destroy him by the Spirit of the mouth of Christ[2] and restore the full teaching of His Son. For so difficult a task, then, God raised up Luther. At the same time, He armed him through the Holy Spirit with exceptional knowledge of Holy Scripture; with singular strength of faith, which stood like an immovable rock in his heart; and with a powerful capacity for teaching and convincing. He set his soul on fire with most ardent zeal for the house of God and filled it with utter disgust for the pope and all godlessness. Further, He opened to him an audience of listeners in a great part of the Holy Roman Empire, not to mention other kingdoms and nations. He defended him and his cause gloriously up to the very last day of his life. Indeed, God Himself has brought it to pass that Luther successfully undertook, more successfully carried out, and most successfully completed the mission which God commanded him, no matter how the gates of the world and of hell raged against him.

Of all the many extraordinary testimonies and successes with which God blessed this His prophet, the following accomplishment should hardly be numbered in last place. When the fortunes of Luther himself and all that he taught seemed especially in jeopardy (no less than they are in this time of ours), because his supporters in the

1 Johann Walter (1496–1570) referred to Luther as "God's prophet true elected, the third Elijah, whereof none hereafter is expected" in his 1564 hymn "New Spiritual Song about the Blessed, Precious, and Highly Gifted Man, Dr. Martin Luther" (AE Bio, p. 98, stanza 59). Johann Mathesius (1504–65) also made reference to this appellation in his biographical sermons on Luther's life: *History of the Origins, Doctrine, Life, and Death of the Reverend, Blessed, Precious Man of God, Dr. Martin Luther* (1566), see AE Bio, pp. 555, 574, 583, 592.

2 2 Thessalonians 2:8.

then-nascent cause were few and weak while his enemies were very many and very powerful—and besides this they had joined together and pledged not to rest until they made Caesar[3] acquiesce to their madness—and though they were prepared to spend their wealth and their life to utterly extirpate this entire teaching, then it was that God further roused the spirit of a few princes and cities to present as their own confession before a diet of the entire Holy Roman Empire articles of the doctrine brought to light through Luther. |This they did at their own great risk. But God so wonderfully governed the affair that these lowly sheep, by this confession of the truth alone, promptly shut the jaws and mouths of the wolves who opposed them.[4]

For when their theologians were ordered to write a confutation of the confession given by these few Lutherans, they undertook the project not only with difficulty and timidity but also with such incompetence and such ignorance of the true foundations of God's Word that this *Confutation*, once it was written down and sounded in the ears of those in the imperial diet (who were waiting for a clear refutation of the alleged heresy), proved rather to witness to the emptiness of papistic doctrine.[5] Nor did they dare, despite our princes' entreaties, let this *Confutation* see the light of day.[6] The final result was that these priests of Baal confessed, when their own princes demanded an accounting, that the Lutheran religion could not be opposed with the Word of God, but perhaps could be opposed using the church fathers instead.

These and many other similar occurrences happened in the way we just described at the Diet of Augsburg, which was held twenty

3 I.e., Emperor Charles V.

4 On June 25, 1530, at the Diet of Augsburg, the Lutheran princes presented the Augsburg Confession to Emperor Charles V. Written by Philip Melanchthon, the Augsburg Confession simply and clearly confesses the Christian faith in twenty-eight articles. It remains the standard of confession in the Lutheran Church to this day. For the text of the Augsburg Confession, see *Concordia*, 27–63; *BoC*, 30–105.

5 Read at the Diet of Augsburg on August 3, 1530, the *Confutation* proved underwhelming, but for Charles V it was enough to suffice as the Roman Catholic refutation of the Augsburg Confession. For the text of the *Confutation*, see *SC*, 105–43.

6 Although their requests to obtain a copy of the *Confutation* were denied, the Lutherans took what proved to be remarkably accurate notes as it was read, and Melanchthon wrote a response: the Apology of the Augsburg Confession (*Concordia*, 73–251; *BoC*, 109–294). The actual text of the *Confutation* was not published until 1559.

years ago already.[7] And the events are well-known to very many people, who were either there themselves or have read the accounts of others.[8]

Therefore, as it was from the beginning, so also then at that diet and in every subsequent public debate, Luther's cause has been victorious. And it remains unconquered still today, supported by the testimonies and proofs of God's Word.

The truth, moreover, is not conquered by strength of arms. Military victory cannot change a thing about the truth. Neither does it always accompany the truth. We know that the deaths of the prophets, of Christ, and of the apostles were all alike and for a like cause. We know that it is God's plan that we, through suffering unjust violence, crosses, and death, may be conformed to the image of His Son.[9] And so the enemy's recent victory should not give them occasion to condemn Luther's cause or to be overly haughty, nor should it lead the pious to be overly distressed.

The cause of the prophets, of Christ, and of the apostles first truly began to come to light in their oppression, and they themselves became more glorious after their death. For this purpose, in fact, God appointed His prophets and apostles, that they might go forth and bear fruit, and that their fruit might remain, that He Himself might work power from their weakness, life from their death, glory from their shame, and planting from their being uprooted.

|And so Luther himself also, though dead, lives to eternity, and the fruit of his work, like the dead man himself, as it were, lives, will live, and will shine to all ages, among still more nations. Nor will the Antichrist ever regain his former strength, no matter how he tries, as Daniel, Paul, and John all testify.[10]

---

7 The Magdeburg Confession was published on April 13, 1550, almost exactly twenty years after the Augsburg Confession was presented (see above, p. 46 n. 4).

8 The German version adds a citation of Luther's *Warning to His Dear German People* (1531) as another witness to the events of the Diet of Augsburg. See AE 47:3–55.

9 Romans 8:29.

10 See Daniel 9:27; 2 Thessalonians 2:5–12, especially verse 8 (ESV): "And then the lawless one will be revealed, whom the Lord Jesus will kill with the breath of His mouth and bring to nothing by the appearance of His coming." Lutherans also read God's sending of the angel of Revelation 14:6, the angel of the "eternal gospel," to be God raising up Luther to preach the Gospel.

The confession of Luther's doctrine, which is the doctrine of Christ Himself, was first made in Augsburg by the confessors in great faithfulness and honor. But now in the same Augsburg it has been cast away, in horrific sin against conscience, by most of the German princes and states, after they were crushed by the single outcome of the latest war.[11] They should have been publicly accused of this public sin, both individually by their pastors and collectively by their rulers, and they should have publicly shown proofs of true repentance. As long as this does not happen, they have left themselves no place for pardon before God, nor will the plague be removed from the families of the princes or from the rest of apostate Germany.

|Or is this not a rejection of the articles of the Augsburg Confession, to subject her very doctrine and church to decrees of a future synod, issued by her known enemy and persecutor? To grant to the enemies and persecutors of this doctrine and church the right to enforce the Interim? To subscribe as commanded to the Interim, resulting in the manifest oppression of the doctrine of Christ and the restitution of the Antichrist? That no more mention should be made of the Augsburg Confession either by word or by writing, but that the memory and appearance of this confession be buried and replaced by its opposite both in name and in the appearance of adiaphora?[12] That this confession be cursed by some to the gratification of the enemy and the injury of the Gospel? That though Luther was the chosen instrument of God to reveal the true doctrine against the Antichrist, yet now Christ's churches are themselves subject to this very Antichrist?

---

11 The alliance of Lutheran princes (the Smalcaldic League) was crushed by Emperor Charles V at the Battle of Mühlberg on April 24, 1547. The emperor then imposed the Augsburg Interim on Lutheran lands in Germany. All resistance was punished severely. The Augsburg Interim, written by a committee of Roman Catholic and Lutheran theologians, was a religious confession and policy that was Roman Catholic in content, conceded authority to pope and councils, and condemned the doctrine of the Augsburg Confession. It was published May 15, 1548. The text can be found in *SC*, 146–82.

12 Adiaphora, or "indifferent things," refer to practices that are neither commanded nor forbidden by God. But because the Interim commanded Lutherans to follow certain practices that reflected Roman Catholic teaching and gave the impression that Lutherans had reverted to Roman Catholic doctrine (e.g., the sacrifice of the Mass, the primacy of the pope, the Corpus Christi festival), faithful Lutherans refused to adopt them. The controversy was later addressed in the FC X, "On Adiaphora" (*Concordia*, 597–602; *BoC*, 635–40).

In all these matters, there is a real rejection of the entire Augsburg Confession and with it also a rejection of Christ Himself. The emperor with his bishops and priests interprets these matters in no other way, nor can our churches, especially the churches beyond our borders, interpret them in any other way. And so very many good men are themselves now being encouraged to reject the doctrine of these articles. And the enemy has been emboldened to further blaspheme and persecute it.

Therefore, although these states and those who join them in their fall from the faith have all truly rejected the Augsburg Confession, and so long as they continue in its rejection and this fornication with the Antichrist,[13] they have made Christ, the Gospel, and whatever remains of Christian worship completely useless to themselves, just as other fornicators with this world do, so long as they do not repent, nevertheless there remains still a poor remnant of states, however weak they may be, and of other godly men, even in the apostate states, who are of one mind with us in this matter, who also hold to the articles of doctrine handed down to us by the ministry of Luther and thereby confess Christ, like the thief on the cross.[14]

Since among these is also our magistracy and our church, the church of this city, so that, in fact, the enemies themselves brag that in attacking us they are attacking the last of this confession, we have determined that it belongs to our office, since we seem by the singular kindness of God to have a voice still free to speak for the whole church, that we publicly set forth something for the purpose of vindicating in some way the revealed doctrine of the Gospel against this unjust oppression.

In the first place, then, we will in this work simply repeat (we will not debate at this time) the chief articles of doctrine proclaimed by Luther and set forth at Augsburg as Christian, orthodox, catholic, and still unrefuted truth, agreeing with the teaching of the prophets and apostles; the Apostles', Nicene, and Athanasian Creeds; and with the purer church of all times. In this connection, we will sometimes add in passing where this constant consensus of doctrine has been

13 Revelation 17:1–2.

14 Luke 23:39–43; the German adds: "He, the Lord Christ, remains on the cross, and we with Him."

abandoned by the Papists, Interimists,[15] and Adiaphorists,[16] as well as by the Anabaptists, Sacramentarians, and similar fanatics,[17] from all of whom we separate ourselves as far as possible.

In the second place, we will demonstrate that the preservation of this doctrine is the duty of a godly magistrate and that its defense by a godly magistrate is just, even if it means a lower magistrate opposing a higher magistrate, when this higher magistrate attempts by force of arms to compel rightly instituted churches of Christ to depart from the known truth and cede to idolatry.

In the third part of this little book, we will warn all the faithful of all churches, both magistrates and subjects, and we will demonstrate not only how great a crime they have committed who have brought aid against us to the persecutors of this doctrine and church, but also how they are not without fault who have failed to lend us their aid, and how each of these offenses, the attack against us as well as the desertion of us, will be perilous to their temporal well-being and their eternal salvation, as well as to all their posterity.

In treating these issues, since we have no wish to insult anyone, we will happily spare the persons doing the harm, as much as the nature

---

15 "Interimists" is the name applied to those Lutherans who agreed to the terms of the Augsburg Interim.

16 "Adiaphorists" is the name applied to those Lutherans who followed a compromise document, dubbed the "Leipzig Interim" by its detractors. Although never officially adopted, the compromise document drafted at Leipzig presented the faith in Lutheran terms (though still compromising on the doctrine of justification) but agreed to use the ceremonies of the Roman Catholic Church. The promoters of the Leipzig Interim, including Melanchthon, argued that they could adopt the ceremonies and practices of the Roman Catholic Church without adopting its actual teachings. For the text of the Leipzig Interim, see *SC*, 183–96.

17 Sixteenth-century Anabaptists rejected infant Baptism and insisted on the exercise of rigorous discipline within the Christian community and strict separation from the wicked: see, e.g., the Schleitheim Confession, Articles 2 and 4, in Lowell Zuck, ed., *Christianity and Revolution: Radical Christian Testimonies 1520–1650* (Philadelphia: Temple University Press, 1975), 72–75. Cf. Luther, *Concerning Rebaptism* (1528), AE 40:225–62. "Sacramentarians" such as Ulrich Zwingli, Andreas Bodenstein von Karlstadt, and their followers, rejected the presence of Christ's body and blood in the blessed bread and wine of the Lord's Supper. Luther grouped Sacramentarians and Anabaptists together with radical spiritualists such as Thomas Müntzer under the epithet of "fanatics" [*Schwärmer*] or "Enthusiasts"—those who rejected the spiritual power of the external Word or Sacraments. See, e.g., Luther, *Against the Heavenly Prophets* (1525), AE 40:79–223.

of the matters concerning which we need to speak allows and as far as the consideration of our duty allows us to be spare in our sparing.

If anyone still thinks something has been spoken too harshly against himself or against others, let him only consider what the issue is and that we must, according to our calling, put the glory of God above the glory of men, just as he himself ought to do in his calling; and that we must hold the eternal salvation of souls more important than the fleeting safety of the body; and that the preservation of His few members is more precious to Christ than all the rest of the world of unbelievers, together with all their trappings and gifts.

CHIEF ARTICLES OF CHRISTIAN DOCTRINE

TO set forth a shorter summary, we will now arrange all Christian doctrine under seven headings.

1. On God and the distinction of persons [in the divine essence].[1]
2. On creation, on the cause of sin, and on the principal kinds of sin.
3. On the Law.
4. On the Gospel and justification.
5. On the sacraments.
6. On the church and her ministers, and on the authority of the church and her ministers.
7. On government and household, and on the authority of each.

The rationale for this arrangement is this:

All knowledge of God is either knowledge of His nature or of His will, which is made known either in creation or in the revealed Word, and this especially so that by this revelation the church may come into being by the ministry of the Law and the Gospel and the sacraments, through men called to this ministry. And both the household and government ought especially to serve this coming into being of the church, or at least to serve the civil interaction of men among themselves, when they fail to attain to the former goal.

But because we are here setting forth only a short and simple explanation of the articles of doctrine as a confession of our faith, we refer the reader to the many writings of the man of God, Dr. Martin Luther, and of other writers like him, from whom you can find a more

1 The German adds the bracketed words here.

thorough treatment and the firm foundations of the faith. And we ourselves, as often as we need to, are prepared to set forth the sources and true foundations of this entire doctrine and of our confession from the prophetic and apostolic Scriptures, as the consensus of the ancient and purer church and of nearly all ages.[2]

Chapter 1: On God and the Distinction of Persons [in the Divine Essence]

On the nature of God we believe and teach from the sure Word of God in accordance with the Apostles', Nicene, and Athanasian Creeds, and in opposition to ancient and modern heresies, that there is one God, Father, Son, and Holy Spirit, that is, three persons, undivided, intelligent, incommunicable,[3] of the same eternal essence, power, and glory, equally from eternity.[4]

We further confess that the Son was made man, conceived by the Holy Spirit, born of the virgin Mary, so that our Lord Jesus Christ is true God and true man, His body and rational soul so united with the eternal Word of the Father in one person, that by this union Christ is God and man. Yet by His free and willing humiliation and inanition[5] He truly suffered, was crucified, died, and was buried, descended into hell according to the will of the Father, rose to life on the third day, ascended into heaven, and sits at the right hand of His heavenly Father, reigning in equal power with the Father to all eternity, until He comes with majesty to carry out the universal judgment of all mankind. Then, when all the dead have been raised, He will render to each according to their works. That is, to those who have repented and believed in Him, He will hand over the possession of the inheritance of eternal life with God. But the rest, the unrepentant and unbelievers, together with all demons, He will subject to the punishments of damnation and eternal death.[6]

---

2 Matthias Flacius would publish his *Catalog of Testimonies of the Truth* in 1556 (*Catalogus testium Veritatis* [Basel: Oporinus, 1556]) largely to argue for this point, that the Lutheran teaching was not novel but continued in the consensus of the ancient and purer church.

3 The incommunicable attribute of the Father is that He is unbegotten; of the Son, that He is begotten; of the Holy Spirit, that He proceeds.

4 Cf. AC I, "On God" (*Concordia*, 31; *BoC*, 36–37).

5 Philippians 2:7.

6 Cf. AC II, "On Original Sin" (*Concordia*, 31–32; *BoC*, 36–39).

Chapter 2: On Creation, On the Cause of Sin, and What Sin Is

Through this Son, our Lord Jesus Christ, God created all things in the beginning, both material and spiritual substances, not from any preexisting matter, but by His command alone, all so that He might in this way manifest Himself and be worshiped. Thus things both exist and are preserved today by the power of the Holy Spirit, the giver of life.

| And although when God created all things, they were at that time very good, yet soon afterward evil crept in, that is, sin and death—not indeed from God, but from the will of the devil and man. For although they[7] had been created in the image of God, for wisdom, righteousness, and eternal life, possessing by nature the freedom to do good according to the will of God, they soon used this same freedom for evil against God and so destroyed themselves, while God simply did not force another outcome or coerce them to act otherwise.

This, we understand, is what happened in the case of mankind:

When our first parents were persuaded by the devil and had eaten from the fruit of the forbidden tree, God was angry and turned Himself away from them according to His righteous judgment. And because of this turning away of God's grace and aid, all the gifts He had placed within man and within the rest of creation were diminished and put into confusion, all because of man's sin. Then there followed upon this loss and disorder of God's gifts also movements of the soul contrary to God. And the devil now obtained power over man and over this fallen world, spread further destruction on our largely forsaken human nature, increased darkness in man's mind, rebellion against God in his heart, and disorder[8] in the lower powers that remained to him. And so God immediately punished sin with sin, with the power of the devil, with calamities of every kind in body and in soul, and, finally, with death. That is, because of sin, man became subject to bodily and eternal death.

---

7 Latin: *Hi*, that is, "they," which should refer to both the devil and man (which is explicitly what the German says: "God created both the devil and man in His own image"). The context calls for the same in the Latin text, since mankind is singled out for explanation in the next paragraph (contra *AS* 476 n. 20).

8 Greek: ἀταξίαν.

Since after the fall into sin our first parents were now such as we have described, they produced no children except ones that were like them, according to their image, not according to the image of God. More than this, the gifts still left in their corrupted nature generally degenerated further in the propagation of the next generations.

Therefore, all men since Adam who are naturally propagated into this life are conceived and born with sin, that is, they are born deserving of the wrath and judgment of God and subject to the power of the devil and death, both because of the actual transgression of our first parents and because of their own corrupted nature. Because of this, they are devoid of true knowledge, fear, faith, and love of God and neighbor; they have become lovers of themselves, full of false ideas, arrogance, disbelief, doubt, hatred of God, evil desires, and words and works opposed to God. Thus nothing is left in all of man, naturally propagated, in any part of him, with which he can either please God or receive grace and life from Him.[9]

Natural[10] man can still in some way produce civilly respectable works. Hence the shadows of virtues and the external discipline seen even among the pagans.[11]

The Papists hold to two errors that are especially opposed to this whole doctrine:

First is the error of denying that the vice inherent in human nature, its deficiencies and its concupiscence, is sin in itself, but is, as they say, the punishment for sin and the tinder for sin, which inclines us to sin and readily gives birth to sin.[12] Their second error concerns the supposed goodness of our depraved nature, that man himself can by his bare natural powers either satisfy the Law of God or merit grace by congruent merit.[13]

9 Cf. AC II, "On Original Sin" (*Concordia*, 31–32; *BoC*, 36–39).

10 Greek: ψυχικός, alluding to 1 Corinthians 2:14: "Natural (ψυχικός) man does not receive the things of the Spirit of God, for they are foolishness to him, and he cannot know them."

11 Cf. AC XVIII, "On Free Will" (*Concordia*, 40–41; *BoC*, 50–53).

12 The Roman Catholic doctrine on original sin, reaffirmed at the Council of Trent in its fifth session, held on June 17, 1546, teaches that concupiscence, that is, the innate inclination toward sin, is not itself sin in those who have been baptized (Denzinger, no. 792; cf. *AS* 478 n. 28).

13 Congruent merit or merit of congruence is merit measured according to the capacity of the human will, for "it seems congruous that God should reward the man

Chapter 3: On the Law

As God has from the beginning made Himself known through His creation, so also has He made Himself known by His revealed Word, both before and after the fall of man, through both commands and promises, given so that man might exercise obedience and faith toward God. Yet His will, which was naturally written on the hearts of man but was obscured as time progressed in the first several generations, God afterward set forth again by giving the Law through Moses,[14] so that man might have for all time the sure testimony of God's Word, from which they might know what they ought to do, what they ought not to do, and what kind of people they ought to be toward God and toward one another. That is, they should be pure of heart, presenting to God a constant and complete obedience, both outwardly and inwardly, without any evil thoughts or feelings. He adds also a promise to those who render this obedience, the promise of eternal salvation in this and in the future life. But to those who sin against Him, He threatens temporal and eternal punishment.

But God did not want this revelation of His will in the Law to serve the purpose that men, by doing the Law, could obtain righteousness and life through the works of the Law or that they should strive to do so, but rather so that despairing of their own merits and terrified at the sight of their sins and the anger of God against their sins—no, more than this, having been put to death by the Law—they might seek and receive from the Gospel the freedom from sin, God's wrath, and death that Christ has won, and thus have righteousness and life through the same. Afterward they should be eager to show their thanks by their obedience to these very commandments. Those who have been justified by faith are reborn through the Holy Spirit in order to begin this obedience to some extent.[15]

It is God's will also that the godless and unbelievers be ruled by outward discipline in this civil society. To this end, He has ordained

---

who works according to his ability" (Thomas Aquinas, *Summa* I–II, q. 114, art. 3). Johann Eck (1486–1543), a leading Roman Catholic theologian during the time of the Reformation, states: "By doing what is in himself a man prepares himself *de congruo* for grace. . . . Man therefore has the ability to make it so that he has eternal life through congruent merit" (*Chrysopassus* 3.60 [CR 1:98]).

14 See Exodus 20:1–17; Deuteronomy 5:6–21.

15 Cf. AC VI, "On the New Obedience" (*Concordia*, 33–34; *BoC*, 40–41).

punishments and rewards of different kinds and either executes them through ministers of the Word, magistrates, and fathers of households or, failing these, He Himself punishes the arrogant in various ways and blesses upright men in this life, so that in this way He may create and retain some discipline in the outward social interaction of life.

Although God did give, besides the Ten Commandments, certain ceremonial and civil laws through Moses, these laws were imposed only on a certain people and for a certain period, up to the time of Christ. They do not obligate Christian churches except insofar as there are elements of natural law in them. But the Ten Commandments are eternal laws. They obligate all men of all times, whether Christians or unbelievers, as we said before.

The Papists hold to many very serious errors against this doctrine of the Law.

1. They corrupt the Law by asserting that lack of fear, faith, and love and similar defects in the nature of man are not sin; likewise, by teaching that man can satisfy the Law of God as far as the substance of the act is concerned and that God is content with outward discipline.
2. They pervert the Law when, out of commands concerning not taking vengeance, concerning giving up one's possessions, and the like, they make "counsels" and works of supererogation and perfection;[16] also when they prefer the self-chosen works of monastic life and other works of human tradition to the works commanded by God's Law. |And although the Interimists and Adiaphorists are not yet advocating these works, yet because they are restoring these very works of human tradition, they are also pretty well confirming the authority by which these

16 The Roman Catholic category of evangelical counsels, which go above and beyond what God requires of normal Christians, include obedience, poverty, and chastity. The "counsels" were kept by priests and monks and so produced works of "supererogation," that is, works that more than obeyed the Law and therefore provided merit also for others. Cf. AC XXVII 12, "On Monastic Vows": "They even added that the monastic life not only merited righteousness before God, but even greater merit, since it was said that the monastic life not only kept God's basic law but also the so-called 'evangelical counsels'" (*Concordia*, 54; cf. *BoC*, 83).

godless opinions arose and so also promoting the godless opinions themselves.[17]

3. The Papists teach the godless doctrine that the Law was given for justification and life, that is, so that we might be justified before God and merit eternal life by the works of the Law.
4. Just as the Anabaptists on their part abolish the Law by doing away with a magistracy, courts, and the distinction between the kingdoms,[18] so the Papists mutilate it and deform it by forbidding marriage to priests and denying that political and domestic occupations are worship when they are carried out by believers.[19]
5. While in this, our time, certain fanatics have wickedly attempted to bring the civil laws of Moses back into the churches of Christians, as if by divine authority,[20] and while the popes of Rome have also instituted their own cheap imitation[21] of the ceremonial laws with the pontificate and the continual sacrifice of the Mass,[22] so, on the other hand, the Antinomians have wanted, in a pernicious display of godlessness, to remove the proper and chief function of the moral law from the church, namely, the

---

17 That is, by adopting Roman Catholic practice and terminology, the Lutherans who go along with the Augsburg Interim (Interimists) or the Leipzig Interim (Adiaphorists) are also promoting the doctrine behind these practices.

18 The Anabaptists taught that God forbade Christians to hold positions in the government or to participate in civil courts. By doing so, they did away with the kingdom of the left (government) and subsumed it into the kingdom of the right (the church). See AC XVI, "On Civil Government" (*Concordia*, 39–40; *BoC*, 48–51).

19 Cf. AC XXIII, "On the Marriage of Priests," and AC XXVII, "On Monastic Vows" (*Concordia*, 46–47, 53–57; *BoC*, 62–68, 80–91).

20 Luther famously addressed the use of Old Testament civil law for Christians in his 1525 sermon *How Christians Should Regard Moses* (AE 35:157–74). See also Luther, *Sermons on Exodus 19–20* (1525), AE 62:311–418; *Sermons on Exodus 20–34* (1525–27), AE 63:9–153.

21 Greek: κακοζηλίᾳ.

22 The Roman Catholics defended their interpretation of the Lord's Supper as a daily sacrifice offered to God by analogy with the Old Testament priesthood, in which the priests offered sacrifices to intercede between the people and God. This is the "cheap imitation" of Old Testament ceremonial law referenced here.

function by which the moral law accuses, terrifies, and condemns those who sin against conscience.[23]

Chapter 4: On the Gospel and Justification

The Gospel is the teaching concerning God's will toward us in Christ Jesus. This will, which was first set forth in Paradise after the fall of our first parents,[24] God Himself subsequently reiterated and made clear, first through the prophets and finally through His Son,[25] that through Him and on account of Him alone He freely wills to receive all who repent and believe in the name of the Son.

There are therefore two parts to this doctrine. One concerns the benefits of Christ themselves. The other concerns the reception of these benefits. The benefits of Christ themselves are, in summary, as follows: that by His merit alone we have freedom from sin, from the wrath of God, and from death, and that we receive righteousness, adoption, the Holy Spirit, and eternal life. The reception of these benefits happens by faith alone in adults who repent, which happens in the following way.[26]

When God forgives or does not impute sin to a man, according to His will, then there is simultaneously joined to this forgiveness freedom from the penalty of eternal death, just as in a court the forgiveness of guilt has joined to it forgiveness of any civil penalty.

---

23 Antinomianism, the teaching that even the moral law no longer applies to Christians, who should be ruled instead by the Gospel, was advanced by the Lutheran theologian Johann Agricola (1494–1566) and vigorously opposed by Luther in a series of six disputations, held between 1537 and 1540, known as the *Antinomian Disputations* (AE 73:3–238). Agricola was a primary writer of the Augsburg Interim. His position was later condemned in FC V and VI, "On Law and Gospel" and "On the Third Use of the Law" (*Concordia*, 484–87, 552–61; *BoC*, 500–503, 581–91).

24 Genesis 3:15.

25 Cf. Hebrews 1:1–2; John 5:39–40.

26 The addition of the phrase "in adults" reflects the Lutheran refusal to speculate on the nature of infant faith, in particular the use of reason and the capacity for intellectual understanding in infants. While Lutherans confessed infant faith, they refrained from psychological or rational arguments as to its creation (cf. AC V [*Concordia*, 33; *BoC*, 40–41]; LC IV 55, 57 [*Concordia*, 728, 729; *BoC*, 463, 464]). The German text of the Magdeburg Confession makes this clear: "The enjoyment of these great goods and gifts takes place only through faith, in righteous repentance, which happens in the following way in the case of those who have grown up and attained to the use of reason."

But in the case of God's judgment, more happens. To those who have been absolved from guilt and eternal punishment because of the Son, God also at the same time imputes all the righteousness of the Son, that is, He declares that they have all the virtues of the Son, and so are righteous before Him with a righteousness of another, as if it were their own. In the same way, when it comes to taking away their guilt and their eternal punishment, God receives the satisfaction of another, of the Son, exactly as if they had each individually accomplished their own satisfaction. |As to this second benefit, although a judge cannot provide this to a guilty man, even if that man is absolved, to declare him, who just a short time before had been guilty of great crimes, in like manner righteous, that is, decked out with all virtues, yet he *can* adopt him as a son. And this is exactly what God also does. He adopts as sons those whom He receives into His grace.

And so those who have been absolved from sin and eternal punishment are at the same time righteous before God with the imputed righteousness of the Son, and they themselves are also sons of God; and they have the right to life and eternal salvation. And this for a twofold reason. First, they have by adoption an inheritance. For sons of God are inheritors of eternal life. Second, they have it just as if they deserved it, because they have the reward of a righteousness not their own but of another, the righteousness of Christ. For life is given, as has been promised, even on account of the righteousness of the Law, as the saying declares: "He who does them, shall live by them" [Leviticus 18:5; Galatians 3:12]. Christ has done this righteousness and has given it to us by imputation through faith. Therefore, we also have life by this imputation of His righteousness.

Moreover, God absolves no one from sin and death, makes no one righteous, calls no one His son and an heir of eternal life without first giving him the Holy Spirit through the Word and Sacraments. The Spirit moves and urges the heart to a true knowledge or taste of sin and the wrath of God, and then to trust in Christ as Mediator, a trust that takes hold of these benefits in Him according to His promise: the forgiveness of sins, righteousness, adoption, and life.

|By this trust alone, moreover, the heart itself is made alive with eternal life, takes in a new and true comfort, light, hatred of sin, love of righteousness, and new strength to resist sin and to do works of inherent righteousness according to the Law. Not that through these works a man is first justified before God, since he is righteous before

this, by the righteousness of another, the Son of God; nor that he can do works that are pleasing to God unless he is first justified in the way just mentioned; nor even that he merits life by these works, since he has the right to this life before he does any work, because he is a son and is righteous with the righteousness of the Son of God. Rather, the believer does good works in order to pay the obedience and honor that are due to God for the kindness of creating and redeeming him in His Son and in order not to lose the benefits he has received and fall back into the wrath of God and death. And so Christ Himself by His Word and Holy Spirit, who works through the Word and the Sacraments, begins regeneration in adults, urges it forward and completes it, so that just as all glory belongs to Him in regard to the merit of our salvation and His giving of Word and Sacraments, so also in the application of this merit, or in the regeneration that occurs in repentance, the beginning, middle, and end is His. This is that "drawing of the Father" of which Christ speaks in John 6:[44].

But the will reborn by the Holy Spirit can use or not use the gifts that it has received. And the gifts themselves increase with the using. And they have bodily and spiritual rewards in this and in the future life. In those who do not use them or who act against them, the gifts that are present are diminished and driven out along with the Holy Spirit. Repeated and constant exhortations are found in the Gospel urging the use of these gifts of the Holy Spirit.[27] | The reborn are commanded by these exhortations to live according to the Spirit, to put to death the works of the flesh by the Spirit, to do works of righteousness.[28]

And although in conversion, or in the regeneration of adults, Holy Scripture describes three principal movements of the soul—namely, contrition, faith, and new obedience—yet these movements work in different ways. Forgiveness of sins, justification, adoption, and life is attributed to faith alone, not to the other two movements, neither by themselves nor in connection with faith. For faith alone receives Christ as Mediator together with His benefits promised in His Word. Therefore, faith alone frees from sin and death, justifies and makes alive, not by reason of its own worth or merit, but because of Christ, on whom alone faith rests and who envelops the whole man.

27 Typical of sixteenth-century usage, the word "Gospel" here simply refers to the entire New Testament, the entire teaching of Christ.

28 Cf. Romans 8:13; Galatians 5:16.

Faith does not therefore exclude contrition and the other virtues, so that they are altogether absent, but it does exclude them from the merit and reception of Christ's benefits, though in such a way that faith itself neither exists nor can exist without them. For faith is properly the justification of the one who knows his own unrighteousness, the consolation of the terrified, the vivification of the conscience slain by the Law when it has seen its sins and the wrath of God against them. Nor does such faith have place or exist in those untroubled by their sin. This faith is also a rebirth to a new and eternal righteousness and life. And without at least the beginning of this new righteousness and life, the faith which boasts of Christ and forgiveness is hypocrisy, not faith; produces death, not life.

|And because this regeneration of the new man only has its beginning in this life through Baptism, and because only the firstfruits of the Spirit are given,[29] not the fullness, therefore the new obedience in its entirety is imperfect. The remnant of the old man remains after Baptism in the sanctified. There remain defects and concupiscence against God's Law, which are real evils and continue to be sin. The apostle, in fact, calls them sin, that is, things that are truly offensive to God and which anger Him.[30] But He is not angry with nor does He therefore condemn the person who believes in His Son, who lives with a good conscience, not according to the flesh but according to the Spirit, just as the judge who absolves a thief nevertheless still despises the crime the thief committed and judges it worthy of hanging and wants the thief he absolved to abstain from thieving in the future, lest he be taken away again to punishment.

I have recited faithfully the sum of Scripture's meaning on the whole matter of justification.[31] Because there are almost infinite corruptions of this teaching among the Papists, we will note only a few, and only the most important, to highlight the difference between our teaching and theirs.

---

29 Cf. Romans 8:23.

30 Cf. Romans 7:7–8.

31 Here, and often elsewhere, the first-person singular suggests a single author wrote the Magdeburg Confession. Although Nicolaus von Amsdorf was the first to sign, most scholars believe Nikolaus Gallus was the primary author (see the historical introduction above, pp. 14–15).

1. First, they have thoroughly transformed the Gospel into the Law by inventing their nonsense about "evangelical commands," that is, commands of the new Law.
2. By taking away the promise of free reconciliation on account of Christ, not only have they done away with the proper distinction between Law and Gospel, but they have also completely erased the proper benefit of Christ and the Gospel. Instead, they have attributed it to their own works, robbed Christ of His glory, and stolen from terrified consciences the comfort they need.
3. But in order not to render Christ completely useless, they have attributed to Him the merit of first grace, by which, absolved of the foreign guilt of our first parents and equipped with the infused habits of faith, hope, and love, we ourselves subsequently merit for ourselves the forgiveness of sins, righteousness, and eternal life by works of the Law, that is, works both of the divine Law and of human traditions.[32]
4. They have taught that first grace is applied to works of penance *ex opere operato*.[33]
5. They have divided penance into three parts—contrition, confession, and satisfaction.[34] And since they attribute to these the merit not only of first grace but also of forgiveness of guilt and punishment, they completely bury faith and Christ.

---

32 Cf. Ap IV 17: "Yet the adversaries do not pass by Christ completely. They require a knowledge of the history about Christ. They credit Him by writing that from His merit a way of life is given to us or, as they say, 'first grace' (*prima gratia*). They understand this as a *habit*, inclining us to love God more readily" (*Concordia*, 84; cf. *BoC*, 122–23).

33 *ex opere operato*, Latin for "by the work performed," that is, without faith being necessary.

34 Pope Eugenius IV (r. 1431–47) issued *Exultate Deo*, a bull of union with the Armenians, at the Council of Florence, November 22, 1439, in which are set forth the three parts of confession as "contrition of the heart, to which belongs both that a person grieves over the sin he committed and the intention of not committing the sin again . . . confession of the mouth, to which belongs the sinner confessing in full all the sins he has memory of to the priest . . . satisfaction for sins, according to the judgment of the priest, which happens especially through prayer, fasting, and giving alms" (cf. Denzinger, no. 699).

6. In confession, they godlessly require the enumeration of all sins as if required by divine right. They godlessly demand also a "sufficient" contrition.[35]
7. They imagine that eternal punishments are turned into the punishments of purgatory for those who are contrite and have confessed their sins They likewise imagine that these punishments of purgatory are paid for by canonical satisfactions, that is, by works of human traditions imposed by the power of the Keys, and, finally, that these very satisfactions can be paid for with money through indulgences.
8. The Augsburg Interim, although it pretends in the chapter "On Redemption through Christ" to attribute all the merit of forgiveness, righteousness, and salvation to Christ and the free mercy of God, yet it subsequently backtracks completely and sets forth individual merit gained through the works of the Law exactly as the Papists teach.[36] For when the righteousness of faith, hope, and love, which Christ merits and which is begun in us through the Holy Spirit, is said to inhere in us and not to free us, justify us, or save us except in its use, and this use is properly our doing, then the glory of our justification and salvation before God belongs to us certainly more than to Christ Himself. No, more than this, if this were the case, we would be justified and saved properly by the works of the Law and not at all by Christ Himself.
9. Both the Papists and the Interimists understand faith here only as the knowledge of the history concerning Christ and whatever else is deemed necessary to know. The fullness and confidence[37] of trust in Christ they completely erase and replace with the opposite teaching,

---

35 Cf. AC XI 1–2, "Concerning Confession": "Listing all sins is not necessary for Confession. For, according to the psalm, it is impossible" (*Concordia*, 37; cf. *BoC*, 44). Here the reference is to Psalm 19:12 (ESV): "Who can discern his errors?"

36 Augsburg Interim III, "On Redemption through Christ Our Lord," states in part: "Although God is gracious to us freely and for his name's sake, and he blots out our sins for his own sake, nevertheless, to show his own righteousness, he does not remit sin without the payment of satisfaction" (*SC*, 150).

37 Greek: πληροφορίαν καὶ παρρησίαν.

commanding people to doubt instead and to rely on the righteousness inside of themselves.

10. The Adiaphorists also depart in many ways from the purity of apostolic teaching and from the Augsburg Confession when it comes to this article. In the first place, while they maintain a distinction between inherent righteousness, or the righteousness of works, or an individual's own proper righteousness as opposed to alien righteousness, namely, the righteousness of Christ imputed through faith, they leave unexplained the chief point of contention in this controversy, and so they confuse these two kinds of righteousness which are so necessary to distinguish.[38] In the second place, when they studiously cast aside the exclusive particle (that a man is justified by faith *alone*) and when they begin now to speak in concert with our adversaries that works are necessary for salvation, they are confirming these two errors of the adversaries: (1) that we are righteous before God by faith in exactly the same way as we are righteous before Him by other virtues we may have; and (2) that our works are meritorious of eternal life. In the third place, they also assert that an individual has some glory of his own before God if he can by some power of his own follow the Holy Spirit when He calls, before regeneration or the moving of the Holy Spirit takes place.
11. Although the Interimists and Adiaphorists make no mention anywhere of the old absurdities about penance, yet the Interimists still retain the structure of all the old abominations; and the Adiaphorists, since they are reinstating all the parts of papistic penance, restoring the bishops as wolves over the churches, and resuming even the papistic ways of speaking of penance, they cannot in the end, even if they wanted to do so, prevent the godless opinions themselves from entering in. Nor will it belong

38 The Leipzig Interim does distinguish between inherent righteousness and the righteousness received by faith, but it sedulously avoids the use of the expression "faith alone" and leaves it unclear whether inherent righteousness is at least part of a believer's salvation, especially since it adopts the expression that good works "are necessary for salvation" (*SC*, 190).

to them to interpret the meaning of these sophistries. That will belong to the adversaries.

12. Concerning the weakness remaining in the saints after Baptism, there is also the manifest error of the Papists, who say this weakness is not sin.[39] Likewise, it is an error when they teach that saints [on earth] can be without sin.
13. We condemn here also the Novatians, who deny repentance to those who have fallen after Baptism.[40] We also condemn the Anabaptists and those like them, who boast of their charismatic gifts and lead men either to new revelations or down other roads and away from the ministry of Word and Sacraments, through which alone God works our salvation.[41]

If anything else whatever conflicts with the teaching about justification as we confessed it above, this also we judge to be utterly foreign to the meaning of Holy Scripture and to stand in the way of Christ's glory and man's salvation.

Chapter 5: On the Sacraments

Together with the Word, the sacraments also serve the reception of the benefits of Christ, which happens by faith alone. The sacraments are, as Augustine says, nothing other than the visible Word. That is, just as the promise of the benefits of Christ is first offered to the ears through the Word, so in turn it is offered to the other senses through the external signs of the sacraments, through which the Holy Spirit is just as efficacious for kindling and exciting faith, so that hearts can believe the promise more firmly, aided, as it were, by these objective signs, and so that individuals can know with certainty

39 See the Council of Trent, June 17, 1546, Session V, Dec. I.5: "This concupiscence, which the apostle sometimes calls sin, the holy Synod declares that the Catholic Church has never understood it to be called sin, as if it were truly and properly sin in those born again, but because it is of sin, and inclines to sin" (cf. Denzinger, no. 792). Cf. Augsburg Interim XV, "On Baptism" (*SC*, 160).

40 Cf. AC XII 9: "The Novatians are also condemned, who would not absolve those who had fallen after Baptism, though they returned to repentance" (*Concordia*, 38; cf. *BoC*, 46). The Novatians were a third-century schismatic group.

41 Cf. AC V 4: "Our churches condemn the Anabaptists and others who think that through their own preparations and works the Holy Spirit comes to them without the external Word" (*Concordia*, 33; cf. *BoC*, 41).

that the promised benefits apply to them, since they have received them in this way. Therefore, the sacraments are not profitable but are actually harmful to anyone who receives them without this faith.

This is the principal and proper use of the sacraments. However, the sacraments are at the same time marks and genuine works of confession by which not only heathen, Jews, and the excommunicated are distinguished from the church, but also within the external society of the church true members can to some extent be distinguished from false ones, that is, from those who despise the sacraments and live like Epicureans.[42]

There are three things that are essential to making something a sacrament. First, the promise of the grace of Christ's benefits. Second, the institution and command of God. Third, the external element and action. These essentials Augustine sums up briefly in the phrase "word and element," when he says, "The word comes to the element, and it becomes a sacrament."[43]

Opposed to this true explanation of the sacraments is the godless teaching of the Anabaptists, by which they deny the true power of the sacraments for salvation and rob them of their true and proper use. Opposed to this true explanation from the opposite side is the error of the Papists, who do attribute efficacy to the sacraments but do so *ex opere operato*, that is, without requiring the trust that clings to the promise and applies the benefits of Christ to the person receiving the sacrament.[44]

There are three sacraments of the kind we just described which have been instituted by Christ in the New Testament. They are (1) Baptism, (2) the Lord's Supper, and (3) Absolution.

On Baptism

Baptism is the washing of water instituted by Christ which takes place in the name of the Father and of the Son and of the Holy Spirit

---

42 Cf. AC XIII (*Concordia*, 38; *BoC*, 46–47). Epicureans are those who live for pleasure, named after the Greek philosopher Epicurus (341–270 BC), who taught that maximized pleasure was the goal of human existence.

43 Augustine, *Tractates on John* 80.3 (NPNF[1] 7:344).

44 Cf. Luther, in his *Assertion* (1520) against Pope Leo X's bull of excommunication: "It is a heretical though common opinion that the sacraments of the new law give grace to those who do not put an obstacle in the way" (WA 7:101).

for rebirth unto eternal life. That is, with this ceremony, as with an eternal pledge, the Father, Son, and Holy Spirit truly make a covenant with the baptized that now all the benefits of Christ apply to him and that he himself belongs to God's people and the true church, is received into grace, is counted righteous, becomes a son and heir of eternal life, and is given the Holy Spirit, who begins the new movements of the new life in his heart, true fear, faith, and love, and who puts to death the desires of the old man.

The outward ceremony itself also depicts these two outcomes. For the washing of water in part signifies the sprinkling of Christ's blood, or the washing away of sins, and in part foreshadows the putting to death of the old man and the birth of the new.

First of all, therefore, we must condemn the Anabaptists, who exclude the poor babies from Baptism either because they excuse them from sinning, as if babies have no sin, or because they point to their faculty of reason, that babies are not yet able to use it or to have faith. We must condemn them also for their repetition of the rite of Baptism, acting as if the first Baptism were ineffective and so diminishing the universal power of true Baptism.

Second, just as in times past the Hemerobaptists,[45] with their opinion that the covenant of Baptism is made ineffective by subsequent sins, would commit the horrible offense of repeating the ceremony over and over again, so now the Papists hold to a similar opinion and commit an offense even more horrible by substituting their own works for the power of Baptism—works, moreover, based not on God's Law but on human traditions, to the point that monks consider their cowls equal to Baptism, even after the monks are dead.[46]

And just as they godlessly remove from Baptism the benefit of forgiving the sins committed after Baptism, so they godlessly add to it another power, which Baptism does not have according to God's Word, namely, the diminution of the original sin that remains in

45 Greek: ἡμεροβαπτίσται; literally, "daily baptizers," people who made Baptism a daily ritual.

46 Compare the statement of the *Exordium Magnum Cisterciense* II.5, a favorable account of the Cistercian order of monks: "Even Judas, had he died in a Cistercian habit, would have gone to heaven." Cf. Luther's comment in *Sermon about Jesus Christ* (1533): "The gray robe and the cowl of the Franciscans take the prize so that whoever is buried in them must go to heaven, whether God likes it or not" (AE 57:125, see also n. 74 there).

human nature after Baptism. Moreover, the true and actual power of Baptism, which belongs to Baptism solely because of God's institution and decree, they attribute directly to the water in a magical way—some on account of a hidden power imparted to the water, others on account of the assistance of the Word.

Finally, with human audacity, they asserted their own sordid inventions into the essential characteristics of Baptism, namely, the practice of magical anointing. And with diabolical blasphemy, they made use of this Sacrament on bells and stones.[47] We disapprove also of the actions of the Adiaphorists, who pollute this Sacrament by reinstituting some of the papistic ceremonies.

On the Lord's Supper

In the Last Supper, Christ set forth His testament for His church, namely, that His true body is to be eaten under the bread and His blood is to be drunk under the wine, a ceremony that is to last until His second coming. By this eating, each Christian is given the opportunity to more frequently remember the Lord in this life, that is, to excite and strengthen his faith by this pledge: that the body of the Lord was handed over and the blood of Christ truly poured out for the forgiveness also of his sins, and that he has become and is a member of Christ and His church and an inheritor of all His benefits. Further, each Christian should by this faith kindle a love toward the other members of the same body, the sharers of this faith, proclaim and praise the Author of such great benefits, and obey Him in this life.

This testament of our Lord Jesus Christ has been contaminated with sacrilege by the Papists:

1. By their mutilation of the institution, by which they rob part of the Sacrament, the chalice, from the greater part of the church.
2. By their repeated and horrible blasphemy, by which they put the Sacrament to uses far different from what Christ instituted, contrary, in fact, to Christ and His merit, namely, in offering it up as a sacrifice not only for the living but also for the dead, to merit for them remission of guilt and of eternal punishment, in purgatory as well

47 They used "holy water" for uses outside of Baptism itself, e.g., anointing bells, gravestones, people.

as in this life, and to obtain bodily and spiritual benefits. They have appointed individual Masses for just about every one of these individual benefits. And then they put the bread in a box and carry it around as a spectacle and object of idolatrous worship.[48]

No better than the Papists are the Interimists, who are offering both kinds of the Sacrament to the laity for a time, not because of Christ's institution but by their own special permission, while they add a clear condemnation of the use of this Sacrament in its wholeness.[49] They adopt an altogether novel opinion and attribute the reception of Christ's benefits and the action of His gracious working (which Christ commanded to happen in eating and drinking) to the sacrifice that happens in the Mass. Finally, when it comes to the eating and drinking or the actual communion, they, together with the Papists, ignore faith and the chief use of the Sacrament.[50]

We disapprove here also of those who concede to the error of the Interimists that the Mass can sometimes be celebrated by the priest alone without any other communicants.[51]

|Finally, we are horrified at the Zwinglians and those like them who deny for whatever reason that Christ can be present or is present and consumed in this Sacrament with the bread and wine, according to His Word, truly, essentially, and bodily. On the other hand, we fault the Papists and Interimists who command us to believe in the transubstantiation of the bread and wine into the body and blood of Christ;[52] likewise, the Adiaphorists, who are now reinstating the

48 The Feast of Corpus Christi, in which the consecrated host of the Lord's Supper is carried out in a box to be adored by the bystanders, is listed as a regular festival in the Leipzig Interim, "On Festivals" (*SC*, 195).

49 Cf. Augsburg Interim XXVI, "On the Ceremonies and Use of the Sacraments": "The whole Christ is contained in each kind" and "Those who practice the use of both kinds should not condemn that ancient practice of communing under one kind" (*SC*, 181).

50 Contrast the Augsburg Interim XIV, "On the Sacraments in General" (*SC*, 159), which does not mention faith, with AC XIII 2, "On the Use of the Sacraments," which states that the sacraments were instituted primarily "to awaken and confirm faith in those who use them" (*Concordia*, 38; cf. *BoC*, 47).

51 Cf. Augsburg Interim XXV, "On the Communion, to Be Joined with Sacrifice" (*SC*, 178)

52 Cf. Augsburg Interim XXVI, "On the Ceremonies and Use of the Sacraments" (*SC*, 181).

elevation of the elements in those places where it had been previously abolished because of abuse or in Christian freedom, as if this practice were necessary on account of the commands of men.[53] Thus they are also confirming the adoration of this Sacrament, especially with the reinstitution of the Feast of Corpus Christi.[54]

We especially condemn this in the Adiaphorists, that they are in large part reinstituting the Papist Mass and so are making the action of this Sacrament into something different from communion, both in fact and in name. In this way, they are opening an obvious door for reinstituting all the papistic abominations.[55]

On Absolution

In the Gospel, Christ gave the authority not only to teach but also to apply the forgiveness of sins and all His other benefits through the Word, either to many or to individuals, as many as seek Him in faith.[56] In the same way, on the other hand, He gave the power not only to teach but also to retain sins, the wrath of God, and damnation on all those who are openly godless and refuse to repent.

And each of these, both absolution and retention of sins, which happens through pastors or through others in cases of necessity, is efficacious in its place not only in the church but also before God. This is because of the institution and Word of Christ, through the Holy Spirit, whom He gave specifically for this purpose and for this assurance, declaring in John 20:[22]: "Receive the Holy Spirit," etc. |And so everyone who receives the Absolution in faith also truly receives forgiveness of sins and the Holy Spirit. Thus Absolution is itself profitable for exercising the faith of individuals.

---

53 Many Lutherans had abolished the practice of elevating the body and blood of the Lord's Supper after the consecration, not wanting to give the impression that the body and blood were being offered to God as a sacrifice or to encourage the adoration of the body and blood outside its being eaten and drunk. The reinstitution of this practice gave the impression that the Lutherans were returning to the practice of sacrificing the body and blood and worshiping the consecrated host, especially when they reinstituted the Feast of Corpus Christi (see above, p. 71 n. 48).

54 See above, p. 71 n. 48.

55 The Leipzig Interim, "On the Mass," begins: "The Mass shall be observed in these lands with bells, lights, vessels, chanting, vestments, and ceremonies" (*SC*, 194).

56 See Matthew 16:19; 18:18; John 20:23.

Confession of sin, which is admittedly instituted by man, does nevertheless serve this Absolution, which is the institution of Christ. Not that absolution cannot take place or is useless without the enumeration of sins, but confession of sin should take place for many other important reasons, in particular because the sacraments should not be given to the unexamined and the unworthy. This is in the interest of everyone's conscience, both the ministers and those receiving the sacraments.

Therefore, just as we condemn the abuse of absolution and confession among the Papists, so we censure certain others for the practice of doing away not simply with the abuse but with the thing itself.

We censure also the Adiaphorists, who, when they speak of Absolution under the heading "Repentance," say nothing about faith but instead add some general remark which, when they explain it, clearly shows that they are adding satisfaction to Absolution.[57]

The Papists and Interimists add other ceremonies to the number of these three sacraments, namely, confirmation, ordination, marriage, and extreme unction.[58] They contend that these have been instituted by Christ and are necessary for salvation just as much as the others. This is a manifest lie. They do not have the promise of the Gospel connected to them so that by them the faithful can apply Christ's benefits to themselves and exercise faith through them. It is this that is the essential characteristic common to the sacraments handed down by Christ.

So also, inasmuch as the Adiaphorists, because of the Interim, fill this number of papistic sacraments as to the outward rites, though they perhaps think differently about the ceremonies themselves, yet because the Interim requires and asserts godless opinions along with these ceremonies, the Adiaphorists are themselves confirming these

57 See Leipzig Interim, "On Repentance," which makes no mention of faith in this article and instead states: "Therefore, they are fervently urged to abandon their sinful way of life and to practice true repentance, prayer, almsgiving, moderation," etc. (*SC*, 192–93).

58 Augsburg Interim XVI, "On Confirmation"; XIX, "On the Sacrament of Unction"; XX, "On the Sacrament of Ordination"; XXI, "On the Sacrament of Matrimony" (*SC*, 160–67).

same opinions, and this not without great danger to the true doctrine and to many consciences.[59]

Chapter 6: On the Church and Her Ministers and On the Power of the Church and Her Ministers

|After the fall of our first parents, God continually proclaimed the promise of Christ, His Son, who would be born of a woman in the fullness of time to crush the serpent's head,[60] so that by the preaching of this promise He might again gather for Himself a church among the human race. Of His own will and judgment, God Himself has always gathered—and will always gather to the end of the world—a people or congregation, sometimes larger and sometimes smaller, to be the guardian of this promise, which both defends against the power of the devil and prevails by the gift of the ministry of Word and Sacraments. Through this ministry, He is always efficacious, again, of His own will and judgment,[61] but only in those of the congregation who hear His Word and receive the sacraments. In them, through the Holy Spirit, He kindles true knowledge, trust in the promised Seed who now has come among us, namely, Christ, and true obedience to Him. He forgives their sins, pronounces them righteous, declares them sons and heirs of eternal life on account of Christ.

Indeed, these alone make up the true church or the true people of God upon the earth, no matter where they are scattered throughout all the world.[62] Their number is now larger, now smaller, but it is always tiny in comparison with the rest of the world. And it is hidden and invisible, because it also has sins and sometimes even errors among its members. And this invisible congregation is everywhere mixed with another much larger congregation, which has the ministry of the Word and Sacraments, sometimes pure and sometimes

59 The Leipzig Interim does not call confirmation, unction, ordination, or marriage "sacraments" but does include them as distinct articles within its treatment of the sacraments, giving the impression that they are in fact sacraments (*SC*, 192–94).

60 See Genesis 3:15; Galatians 4:4.

61 Cf. AC V 2: "The Holy Spirit . . . works faith, when and where it pleases God, in those who hear the good news" (*Concordia*, 33; cf. *BoC*, 41).

62 Cf. AC VII 1, "On the Church": "The Church is the congregation of saints in which the Gospel is purely taught and the Sacraments are correctly administered" (*Concordia*, 34; cf. *BoC*, 43).

less pure. By this ministry, the whole church becomes visible, though in it there are very many evil men. Yet some of them are converted from time to time, and sometimes those who hold governance over the church are themselves enemies of the true church.[63]

But the true members of this true church, though they have the Word and Sacraments in common with the rest of the multitude, shine like stars compared with the others, because they show true obedience to God, and in persecution they make their confession according to their calling, and they suffer when necessary. They are recognized by these things to some extent, but in the end, it is usually after their deaths that those who were truly faithful become clearly known.

To speak specifically of the church of the New Testament, Christ gave her the Keys of the kingdom of heaven, just as He received them from His Father.[64] He did not give them to Peter only or even only to the rest of the apostles and their successors in ministry, but first and foremost He gave them to the entire visible church, so that the Keys might be the proper possession of the true church of the saints.[65]

While the church, for the sake of order, by human decision, later entrusted the administration of the Keys to certain people, she nevertheless retained the complete right of the Keys for herself, if the ministers to whom they have been committed either completely refuse to exercise them or wish to exercise them only for destruction.

She retains also the right to administer the Keys in cases of necessity, as when a sufficient number of ministers cannot be had for indispensable tasks. Otherwise no one has the right to take upon himself the ministry, whether publicly or privately, without a lawful call through men.[66]

Now the power of the Keys is the power of teaching the Word of God, administering the sacraments, loosing and binding the sins of

---

63 Cf. AC VIII 1, "What Is the Church": "Because many hypocrites and evil persons are mingled within them [the congregation] in this life, it is lawful to use Sacraments administered by evil men" (*Concordia*, 34; cf. *BoC*, 43).

64 Cf. Matthew 16:19; 18:18.

65 Contrast Augsburg Interim XIII, "On the Supreme Pontiff and the Bishops": "On the basis of divine right . . . [the church] has one supreme pontiff, set over all the others, with plenitude of power, through the prerogative given to Peter" (*SC*, 158).

66 Cf. AC XIV, "Order in the Church": "No one should publicly teach in the Church, or administer the Sacraments, without a rightly ordered call" (*Concordia*, 39; cf. *BoC*, 46).

individuals or many, calling ministers, identifying and judging questions of religion, and establishing traditions that serve the ministry instituted by Christ.[67] The Keys do, in fact, include the authority to do all these things as a whole and individually, provided that all is done not according to human judgment but according to the instruction of God's Word, for the edification of the church, not its destruction, for the living and not the dead.[68]

Each minister exercises the duties of this office, but he administers those specific duties entrusted to him, and he does it in those specific places where the church, or those whom the church appoints to act in her stead, directs and as God distributes the measure of His grace to each in the office entrusted to him.

So there is this distinction between ministers, but only by human arrangement, where one minister looks after more churches than another, as with a bishop or a superintendent, and one undertakes more or different duties of the ministry than another, as with members of a consistory, pastors, preachers, and deacons. But the idea that one man presides over all these duties and looks after all churches in all the world and has become the universal bishop, this is not handed down to us in the Word of God. No, in fact, it is contrary to the Word of God. It is therefore an impossibility and totally destructive of the church.

Although the talents of ministers are not the same when it comes to administering their duties, and though there are often evil and godless men serving as ministers, yet when they administer the essentials of Word and Sacraments, the worthiness of the minister does not increase the dignity and efficacy of the ministry and his unworthiness does not decrease it.

Against this summary and true explanation stand many abominable errors, of which we will enumerate these few:

First, the error of the Donatists and Anabaptists, who, in their insistence that the visible church consists only in true believers, command Christians to separate from everyone else, even from the congregation that has the pure ministry. But they set up their own

---

67 Cf. AC V, "On the Ministry," and AC XXVIII, "On the Power of Bishops" (*Concordia*, 33, 57–62; *BoC*, 40–41, 90–103).

68 That is, not for the souls supposed to be in purgatory, for whom also the Mass is sacrificed in the Roman Catholic Church.

congregations for themselves in which, they say, all are equally and truly saints.[69]

Second is the error of the Papists, by which they act as if saints in the church are without sin[70] and that they must be under one head and outwardly associated with the Roman pope.

Third, when the Papists speak of saints in the church, they understand dead saints to be almost divine and command us to call upon them in obvious idolatry, to seek help from them, to run to their statues and their relics, and so forth.[71]

Fourth, in contending for the primacy of the Roman pope, there are many outrageous errors. |(1) They make him, by divine right, the bishop over all the church in all the world. (2) They attribute to him alone, by divine right, the power of the Keys, so that he himself receives them directly and all others only indirectly through him. (3) They give him both swords and full power in each kingdom, ecclesiastical and political. (4) They attribute to him power and authority over the Scriptures, to change and make decrees about the Word, sacraments, and commands of God; to establish articles of faith; to institute rites of worship and sacrifices; to change the natures of things; to confer new spiritual power on these things so they give eternal life; to determine questions about faith and morals so that in all these things he cannot err, nor may any man argue with him or think differently concerning his decrees and actions, even if he knowingly leads innumerable souls to hell (Dist. 4, *Si papa*).[72]

On top of this, they give him power not simply over the living but over the dead, and over the angels themselves! Because of these things, instead of being the vicar of Christ, he has truly become the

---

69 Cf. AC VIII 3 (*Concordia*, 34; *BoC*, 42–43), which condemns Donatism, a heresy arising in fourth-century North Africa, which contended that the sacraments of unbelieving priests (priests who had formerly renounced the faith under Diocletian's persecution) were invalid.

70 Greek: ἀναμαρτούς.

71 Augsburg Interim XXIII, "On the Memorial of the Saints in the Sacrifice of the Altar and on the Intercession for Them Required in It, and Also on the Invocation of the Saints": "The merits of the saints serve for salvation not only for them but also for us" (*SC*, 175).

72 While the 1198 papal bull *Si Papa* of Pope Innocent III does argue for the infallibility of the pope and the complete obedience owed to him, it also asserts that he is to be deposed if he is a heretic. Cf. *Decretum Gratiani*, Part I, D. 40, c. 6; and below, p. 103 n. 31.

vicar of the devil and the Antichrist who reigns in the temple of God, as Daniel, Christ, and Paul prophesied of him.[73]

Lastly, the Adiaphorists greatly aid these horrible abominations when they hand over the honor of primacy to the pope, whom they previously condemned as the Antichrist and whom they still utterly condemn in their consciences, and when they take the churches of Christ that had been so happily freed from this wicked demon and force them again under his tyrannical yoke, all by their appeal to "adiaphora," which they use as a kind of magical incantation.[74]

|The Adiaphorists should also be condemned for what they say in the Leipzig Interim, that we must teach what the church orders, though the church ought not to establish religious doctrine but only hear the doctrine received by Christ.[75] In this heading, they are clearly arming the council[76] to fundamentally overturn the true religion, to our great disadvantage.

Chapter 7: On the Government and the Household and the Power of Each

As the church is God's institution, in which God wants there to be an order of those who teach and those who learn, so also government and the household are truly God's institutions, in which He likewise wants there to be an order of rulers and ruled. The ruled should be subject to and obey their rulers' laws and mandates, and these laws and mandates should in turn accord with reason and not conflict with

73 See Daniel 9:27; Matthew 24:15–16; 2 Thessalonians 2:5–12; and above, p. 47 n. 10. On papal claims to being the "vicar of Christ," see the historical introduction above, p. 34, and n. 31 there.

74 The Leipzig Interim uses the excuse of "adiaphora" to justify the adoption of Roman Catholic practice and concession to papal authority: "Accordingly, our first consideration is that everything that the ancient teachers regarded as adiaphora, that is, things that are neither commanded nor forbidden by God, may still be regarded as adiaphora without compromising Scripture" (*SC*, 184). Here the constant use of the word "adiaphora" is compared to the repetition of magical spells. On the pope, the Leipzig Interim concedes that "all other ministers shall be subjected and obedient to the highest bishop" (*SC*, 192).

75 See Leipzig Interim, "On the Power and Authority of the Church," which states in part: "Whatever the true Christian church, assembled in the Holy Spirit, recognizes, determines, and teaches in matters of faith shall continue to be taught and proclaimed" (*SC*, 191).

76 I.e., the Council of Trent.

the Word of God. This they should do not only in view of the wrath and fear of punishment which threatens them from their rulers but also for conscience's sake, that is, in view of the wrath and judgment of God.[77]

For God has armed these His institutions and authorities with fear of each kind—fear of God's wrath and punishment as well as fear of the wrath and punishment of the men who exercise the authority. And in His Word, He has made a distinction between one authority and the other, so that to each of them He attributes a particular scope and office, as well as a particular administration of punishment.

Although He does not want the authorities to be confused with one another, He does want them so to serve one another that in the final result they all harmonize one with the other, and each in its own place and in its own way promotes as of first importance the true knowledge and glory of God and the eternal salvation of its members; or, when it does not attain this ultimate goal, at least effects the secondary goal of men living peacefully, honestly, and beneficially[78] in this life's civil society.

Therefore, governments and households have been instituted by God, and are preserved and defended by Him, principally for the sake of His church. Adults who do not have the gift of celibacy should all enter into marriage according to the word and command of God, should become fathers and mothers of families, should procreate, and should bring up their children and the rest of their household in the instruction and discipline of the Lord, as the apostle says.[79] |That is, they should accustom them to hard work and true piety and correct the disobedient with words and whacks.[80]

The lawfully called magistrate ought, according to God's Word, to defend pious and honest citizens and subjects, and the church in particular, against the violence of evil men. These he should restrain by physical power and the sword. He should make it his greatest concern that people are rightly instructed in religion, and in public and private life encouraged toward true piety and honesty.

---

77 Cf. Romans 13:1–5.

78 Greek: καὶ ὄυκ ἄκαρποι; literally, "and not without fruit" (cf. Titus 3:14).

79 Cf. Ephesians 6:4.

80 Latin: *verbis et verberibus*

Just as it is necessary for subjects to obey their magistrates in these things, and for children and the rest of the family to obey their parents and masters, because God commands it, so, on the contrary, when magistrates or parents lead those under them from piety and honesty, no obedience is owed them as if God commanded it.[81]

When also they openly persecute true religion and honesty, they remove themselves from the office of magistrate and parent before God and before the consciences of those under them, and instead of an institution of God they become an institution of the devil, which can and ought to be resisted according to one's vocation.

Further, since political and household life and authority are both truly God's institutions, the Gospel not only approves of them and allows the pious to use them, but it also sanctifies them, so that the works done in the government and the household, considered altogether or individually, are pleasing to God and are acts of worship toward Him in believers, so long as these works are consistent with the laws of the land and with reason, and so long as they do not conflict with God's Word.

Accordingly, the error of the Anabaptists should be the first to be condemned here. They deny that governmental or household offices are allowed to Christians. They abolish magistracies, courts, ownership of property, contracts, etc., as if these things were evil in themselves.[82]

The error of the Papists is not too much different from this one. They, of course, do not condemn governmental and household affairs, but they do denigrate them to a great extent and shower them with exceeding contempt when they deny that God is worshiped by these kinds of life. They go further and completely deny marriage to an entire class of men, namely, the priests, contrary to God's Word and command. They put asunder this union or else hypocritically permit it only to some. They adorn their impure celibacy, with its abandonment of common duties and the risks of married life, disgusting in its

---

81 Cf. Acts 5:29 (ESV): "We must obey God rather than men."

82 Cf. AC XVI, "Civil Government" (*Concordia*, 39–40; *BoC*, 48–51).

ease, luxury, security, and all impiety, with the title of perfection in a spiritual kind of life.[83]

|Third, just as many consciences of good men were disturbed by the denigration and deformation of governmental and household offices under the papacy, with the result that they thought too lightly of these institutions of God and the majesty of political leaders was trampled underfoot, so, now that dignity has been restored to civil and household authority through the Gospel, some sin in the other direction and think that these authorities are totally sacrosanct and inviolable even when they try to oppress the good work they should be honoring and, on the other hand, establish and honor the evil work to which they should be a terror. This is the subject that we have undertaken to treat more thoroughly in the second part of this little book.

83 Cf. AC XXVII, "On Monastic Vows," especially paragraph 61: "So many wicked opinions are inherent in monastic vows—that they justify, that they cause Christian perfection . . ." (*Concordia*, 57; cf. *BoC*, 91).

EPILOGUE TO THE DOCTRINAL CONFESSION

YOU have now, dear Christian reader, the summary of this doctrine, which is founded on the prophetic and apostolic Scriptures and in these last times has again been retrieved from the great darkness of the Antichrist's reign through Luther, the man of God of holy memory, and has been set forth in the articles of the Augsburg Confession. By the singular kindness of God, this teaching sounds still today uncorrupt and pure in our churches.

If in this exposition, whether when treating the articles of the true doctrine or when addressing ancient and modern false teachings, we have said anything incompletely or imperfectly because of our brevity, our hearers can have a clearer account from our other sermons. As to other readers of this our little book, we would rather them go further and drink more deeply from the writings of Luther as from a great river that flows straight from the very sources and carries gold in its waters, or even from the writings of others like his. We hope, nevertheless, that nothing has been said here or will be understood here different from what these have taught.

We also have ceremonies in our churches that agree with the doctrine of the apostles and with the purer church which followed immediately after the apostles. They are pious and useful for building up the church, as we have received them from excellent churches that are known for true piety. And just as we can change nothing concerning the doctrine of these churches without outrageous insult, denial, and blasphemy against Christ (nor do we intend to, so long as Christ supplies us with strength, which is the very thing we pray and hope!), so we have decided that it cannot be permitted, without the same scandal, for ceremonies to be separated from doctrine in such times and circumstances as ours, nor can there be the appearance of agreement between Christ and Belial,[1] the very thing some are now doing to escape the cross. This has already been clearly shown by our previously published writings, and no one up to this point has been able to argue otherwise—indeed, no one has even dared to touch the heart of this controversy with a response, which provides the best evidence of a bad conscience in a wise and learned opponent.[2]

Therefore, we have now written this confession in our name and the name of our churches and in the name of all outside our walls who are still pious, who have not yet bowed the knee to Baal, whose spirit, prayers, and groans we have no doubt are now joined with ours. We have written this confession, first of all, so that we may give the true witness to Christ, who is now hanging on the cross,[3] and so that we may offer Him our necessary worship, which He Himself now fiercely demands from all; next, so that we may strengthen our brothers in Christ also, wherever they are, by our confession and our example; finally, so that we may free ourselves once and for all from suspicion of novelty or departure from the true doctrine and right worship, we who have done nothing else in this matter than guard that holy deposit of the man of God, Dr. Martin Luther, uncontaminated, for which we now have been proscribed and made offscourings and refuse[4] not only to our enemies but also to our brothers. Just a short time ago, we all considered ourselves blessed to have this deposit! We were blessed indeed. And we boasted in it. But we ourselves consider ourselves still blessed today, and we boast in the cross of our Lord Jesus Christ.[5] Whatever happens in the end, we will die with Christ and we will live with Christ, with His Spirit helping us, since He has promised to give Him as a Helper in time of need to those who seek Him in faith.[6]

---

1 Cf. 1 Corinthians 10:20–21; 2 Corinthians 6:15–16.

2 The opponent alluded to is Melanchthon, the *de facto* leader of the Adiaphorists and one of the authors of the Leipzig Interim.

3 It has been suggested that this wording speaks to the drafting of the Magdeburg Confession during Holy Week (*AS* 530 n. 135). It is also a readily understood biblical expression: "since they are crucifying once again the Son of God" (Hebrews 6:6 ESV).

4 Greek: καθάρματα καὶ περιψήματα (cf. 1 Corinthians 4:13).

5 Galatians 6:14 (ESV): "Far be it from me to boast except in the cross of our Lord Jesus Christ."

6 Cf. John 14:26.

THE SECOND PART OF THIS LITTLE BOOK

On Defense

IF the Interimists and Adiaphorists really are the kind of people most of them want to be considered, men who retain the purity of the teachings set forth above, who even uphold them against the Papists, then they have no grounds to criticize the same purity among us, which they are now hearing from us and learning from the witness of our own actions, that is, from our public sermons and ceremonies.

But if they accuse us of stubbornness because of our refusal to change anything (I will not speak now of adiaphora and how these adiaphora have now ceased to be adiaphora and have instead become sins, denials, and rejections of the faith), with what arrogance and what conscience will they condemn and attack with armed opposition the very ceremonies that they themselves previously commended to us as godly and useful, the very ceremonies they kept and still would keep if they had not been overcome by fear of danger?

This part of our confession and defense, therefore, stands in no need of proof at all for at least this portion of our enemies—the Interimists and Adiaphorists. For they themselves must freely confess that we cannot be justly condemned or attacked by Christians because of our teachings and ceremonies.

As to the Papists, who have always been our enemies, while it is true that neither this simple confession nor any other clear demonstration of the truth can free us from their accusation of heresy against us, still very many among them, convinced by the light of God's Word and their own consciences, know that we have been wronged in this matter. Indeed, they have often confessed this very thing in their disputations and in their other speeches. Certainly, everyone knows and ought to know that according to divine, natural, and human law—yes, even according to the Papists' own treaties and promises—we cannot be condemned and attacked when our case is still unheard, especially since we have constantly begged that our case be heard in a legitimate court.

Although some princes and states have already given up the right to plead their cause, together with the cause itself, any sane observer will be quick to understand that this prejudice cannot and ought not be imposed on others, especially in a matter pertaining to the glory of God and the eternal salvation of all men. Rather, though few and altogether despised, they are still right to demand their right, even if the powerful and the lawless mock it with careless abandon.

But because the enemies themselves cannot but understand the filthy baseness and extreme injustice of their actions, something resembling a righteous fear led them to plan and pursue very carefully the cover-up of this their baseness and to deny that this last war was initiated to suppress our religion before it had a legitimate hearing.[1]

But now, after their victory has been won and they are in control of things and have been made sufficiently powerful, they openly manifest that they are pursuing the oppression of this religion before it is given a legitimate hearing (though they still pretend the ridiculous pretext of our "rebellion" for their suppression of the pitiful remnant of this confession). For they are burdening the regions and cities that have surrendered with extreme injustice, with cruelty unheard of even among the heathen, and with forced changes to their religion, not only through the Interim but also by the restitution of the papacy wherever and however much they can.

Therefore, as far as it pertains to this part of our apology, our magistracy has again decided that it must say something about this defense. The first and only reason for the enemy's hatred, proscription, and now their vile attempt to destroy our city is this: that our City Council took care from the very start, as soon as they had removed all godless teachings and forms of worship from their churches, to establish the true teaching and right forms of worship in these their churches, and then later to do the same with those churches among us

1 Because the Smalcaldic War (1546–47) began with the leaders of the Smalcaldic League, Landgrave Philip of Hesse and Elector John Frederick of Saxony, attacking Duke Heinrich of Braunschweig-Wolfenbüttel, Emperor Charles V argued that the formal cause of the war was political and not suppression of Lutheran teaching and practice.

that had been abandoned by the Papists; and now our City Council is simply unwilling to reject the true doctrine and right forms of worship and to receive again false teachings, idolatries, and blasphemies. To stop all this from happening, it is doing what is necessary for its own defense and the defense of its people.

This, I say, is the first and only reason the enemies have for their attempt to crush this city and for this city in turn to put up its necessary defense. This is so obvious to anyone who honestly considers the matter (even if no one says it out loud at the moment) that there is no reason not to call those people enemies who stood out as the first actors of this tragedy—unless ignoring the judgment of your own conscience and of all right thinking and believing nothing but what you want and what serves your own belly is now considered some sort of noble Epicurean virtue!

|Nor do I think that anyone who knows anything about the condition of this city and its neighbors and its public actions would say that our magistrates are seeking anything but peace and the true religion. They are certainly not trying to rob anyone of his honor or riches!

But I leave this to our City Council to explain, as well as to the judgment of all good men who know even the slightest amount about how our adversaries and the highest magistrates have regarded our religion's cause, its start, its continuance, and its success among the remnant that is truly committed to this confession.

In this our apology, we now need to demonstrate whether a Christian magistrate can or ought to protect his lands, and the Christian teachers and hearers in them, against his higher magistrate, and to repel him by force if he attempts to violently compel his lands into a rejection of the true teaching and right worship of God and into the acceptance of idolatry instead.

We see that a genuine and very simple approach to making our point is open to us when we examine the people before whom we have to treat this question. Among them are the two kinds of enemies whom we have already mentioned above. These are the Papists on the one hand, and on the other the Interimists, and joined with them, the Adiaphorists. But there is a third kind also: those who ought to be making a defense. We are writing so that they may have sure and firm comfort in confronting the dangers of such a defense.

Among these latter two groups, there should clearly be no need of this repetition of the question, since only a short time ago it was crystal clear to most of them, on the basis of genuine proofs from the Word of God and from the natural knowledge divinely impressed on the human mind. Unless perhaps, when it comes to the argument for a lawful defense, the will of the king and his weapons have changed the very concepts of divine and natural law, cause and effect, and all the rules of logic, as they have been able to do in many articles of Christian teaching up to this point.[2]

So, by the same reasoning that two times four will stop being eight, magistrates and subjects will be mutually bound by definite limitations and oaths, but the magistrates will be allowed, whenever they want, to be free and unbound from every obligation, while the subjects will always be bound and never be free. The magistrates will be allowed to exercise extreme tyranny against the laws and their own oaths, but the subjects will not be allowed to lawfully resist the madness imposed by the tyrants. Thus the truth of knowledge and the law of cause and effect will always depend on the whim and arms of those who have more power.

But as to our other enemies, the Papists, we will have proved in vain that the lower magistrate has a right of defense against the higher magistrate if the higher magistrate persecutes the true religion with arms, since they deny that our religion is the true one. They therefore think their war is just, though not even here are they thinking correctly, as we said above.[3]

And so, in setting forth this defense, we especially have regard for the consciences of those who still keep to the pure doctrine, or at least do not want it to be oppressed and persecuted. We want each of these groups to know what they should do in regard to this defense and how they can find comfort in doing it.

But first we appeal to you, Emperor Charles, most merciful lord, not to allow the pope's contingent to so abuse your majesty and authority and expel Christ from your land—oh, even to crucify Him in it! This is the very Christ who gave you the flourishing kingdom you possess. Now He is a stranger in it, poor, cast down and full of

---

2 That is, the emperor's armed enforcement of the Augsburg Interim led many princes and theologians to change their position on basic doctrine, without any theological or logical rationale.

3 That is, even if the Lutheran confession were wrong, it has not been given a fair, legal hearing.

troubles in His members, that is, in His disciples. Now He is testing your faithfulness in administering the kingdom He entrusted to you, not by demanding that part of this kingdom or part of your glory be given back to Him, but only that He be given a defense or at least some safety within it. So He will repay your faithfulness and gifts to Him with greater gifts in the life to come.

But if you are otherwise convinced in your conscience and so cannot yet consider us disciples of Christ, please consider, as your piety allows, that Christ Himself, when He was delivered over to be crucified by the high priests of His people, was not considered to be the Son of God but the opposite, a blasphemer and a rebel. So the apostles and the other martyrs were considered and were likewise butchered by the civil authorities, just as the Lord said would happen: "They will cast you out of the synagogues. Indeed, the hour is coming when anyone who kills you will think he is rendering service to God" (John 16:[2]).

With this sentence, the Lord also shows us the marks of the false church, namely, that it will spread its religion by force of arms. The true church, on the other hand, has never taught that men should be forced by arms to true piety, even as you yourself allow Jewish and heathen parents to practice their religion in your empire. You do not force them to accept your religion by force of arms.[4]

We wretched Christians, because we are called Lutherans, are therefore more miserable than Jews and heathen! Why are we alone deprived of this kindness of yours? We who preach together with you with one mouth and with one heart Christ, our common Redeemer and Savior; we who sincerely embrace all the articles of the Christian faith; we who are separated from you only in this one point, that we seem to you (persuaded as you are by papal influence) to attribute too much merit and glory to Christ in the article of justification, and that we think He should be worshiped only according to His Word, whereas you think He should be worshiped differently and so force us to worship Him according to human traditions.

See, therefore, I pray, august Caesar,[5] how serious a matter this would be for you at the final judgment of Christ, where you will have

4 The *Decretum Gratiani* (the twelfth-century collection of canon law) forbade the forced conversion of Jews (Part I, D. 45, c.7).

5 I.e., Emperor Charles V.

to render to Him an account of all your actions and will receive in turn what your actions deserve, if you being a Christian yourself have been the persecutor of Christians, of the true members of Christ, and that because they seemed to you to extol Christ and His Word with too much praise!

In everything else that belongs to your kingdom, we will willingly render the highest obedience we can, as is our duty. The profession of our religion is far from robbing you of this obedience. In fact, you gain much from it in true dignity and in the aid we render in carrying out the duties of obedience owed to you. | For we teach with Paul that you are a minister who stands in God's place to promote good works, and that therefore to you, as to God Himself, obedience is due, not only because of wrath or fear of the sword but also because of conscience, that is, fear of the wrath and judgment of God.[6]

Although we ourselves cannot hope to have everyone equally obedient to this doctrine or force everyone to it, yet we can promise you this by the power of the promise which is spoken of our ministry—"My word will not return to Me void" (Isaiah 55:[11]) and "Your labor in the Lord will not be in vain" (1 Corinthians 15:[58])—that we will give very many from our churches who will declare their obedience and unfeigned faithfulness to you in all the honest duties that are owed to you, if only they can enjoy their religion peacefully through you. And they will do it not only because they are receiving a benefit from you but out of true love for you, more perhaps than all whom you now say are obedient to you. Therefore, it is an error that you censure us with the accusation of stubborn disobedience and the crime of rebellion.

Although we cannot, of course, peer into individual hearts, we can nevertheless guarantee this concerning the public and common will and intention of this city: we require nothing else except the preservation of our religion. When we obtain this, our City Council and our citizens will be most obedient to your Majesty, in all their proper duties and according to the laws. And if this were not the case, if we did not so clearly see that this is the public intention and will of our church, we would have forced this entire church to desist from the beginning and carried out excommunication according to Christ's command, or else we would have shaken the dust off our feet and left this city ourselves. | For we insist, according to Christ's Word, that the

6 Romans 13:1–5.

things of God be rendered to God and the things of Caesar, even a Caesar of a different religion, be rendered to Caesar.[7]

These duties of twofold obedience mutually serve and aid each other without offense to conscience on either side and without tumult, so long as each stays within the limits prescribed by God and by the laws that govern their office. But when there is a departure on either side, horrible sins and serious tumults necessarily arise—as you now, Emperor Charles, are exceeding the limits of your kingdom and are extending your kingdom into the kingdom of Christ. Therefore, you yourself are the reason for these disturbances, just as Elijah once said to Ahab.[8] Those are not the cause who will not and cannot, out of fear of God's wrath and eternal punishment, pay to you the honor that you have seized away from God.

It only remains, then, that we beseech your Majesty, august Caesar, by the suffering, cross, death, and resurrection of our Lord Jesus Christ, whose remembrance we still adore together with you, and that we urge you by His most righteous and severe judgment to desist finally from outlawing and persecuting us and other innocent Christians, since we are bound and devoted to Christ, who is your Lord and ours.

|If we cannot obtain this from you, as we have been unable up to this point, nor have others been able who acted as advocates for us, then you will surely hear from us an evil testimony before Christ your Judge on the Day of Judgment, and even now our groanings will ascend with the groanings of other pious Christians into the presence of our God. And these will speed your punishment, because you will be forcing righteous men of peace into a necessary defense against your implacable and unrighteous cruelty.

We are not happy at all to have to set forth this teaching about defense, however true it is, since we know that there are very many wicked people in the outward fellowship of the church who can use this pious confession as the pretext to pursue their own godless endeavors, whatever they may be. Besides this, even good men are sometimes affected by their flesh and grow so impatient in enduring injuries that they could very wickedly abuse the judgments we are

7 Matthew 22:21.

8 1 Kings 18:17–18.

correctly setting forth by using them in the wrong place and at the wrong time.

We know also that it is for this reason that the greatest theologians who came before us were extremely cautious, hesitant, and careful in setting forth their judgment on this point, especially when it was not yet necessary to do so, and there was no profit in explaining it to everyone or to those who were curious about it.[9]

But now your Ahithophels[10] are especially intent on destroying us and, after that, on completely wiping out the whole church of pious believers who refuse to consent to their idolatry. Every sane person now understands this.

And to accomplish this horrible crime, they have placed the highest hope in the use of your title and your power, O Emperor. It is by use of your name, as by the thundering of God's wrath, that they want to terrify everyone. Thus they think that out of fear of God's wrath no one will resist them, and that they themselves can safely and easily restore through you the abominable idol of desolation in the temple of God[11] and kill everyone who disagrees with them.

The same thing happened in the time of the Maccabees, when Antiochus took advantage of some who refused to fight on the Sabbath out of a false fear of violating it.[12] So he cruelly slaughtered them all at the same time without any trouble. And he conceived the hope that he could destroy the rest of the people by the same plan and strategy (by taking advantage of their observing the Sabbath), since they held so strongly to the worship that God had commanded them. In this way, he planned to destroy the true worship of God and institute the same religion over all nations, according to the dictates of his own will.

In that same time, Mattathias liberated the consciences of the remaining believers and armed them to "fight for their lives" against

9 Luther, in particular, was hesitant to set forth his judgment on this matter; see below, p. 99 n. 26, and also the historical introduction above, pp. 7–8.

10 A counselor of King David. Ahithophel defected to Absalom, David's son who usurped his throne. See 2 Samuel 15:31–17:23.

11 Cf. Daniel 9:27; Matthew 24:15.

12 This account of Maccabean resistance can be found in 1 Maccabees 2. Antiochus Epiphanes (r. 175–164), the Seleucid king, enforced religious conformity on his subjects and forced the Judeans to sacrifice to pagan gods. Led by Mattathias and his sons, especially Judas Maccabeus, the Judeans revolted and eventually prevailed against him.

the king, as he himself said, and "for the righteous ordinances of their God" [1 Maccabees 2:40], lest they perish completely from the land. Since in our time the same thing is quite obviously being attempted by your Antiochuses and Ahithophels, whom you have among your advisers, we likewise must take into consideration our situation and the peril we face and must liberate the consciences of our people from this empty fear that is thrown in their faces, namely, that God does not allow a defense against higher magistrates. So we must urge our people to be zealous for the law and give their lives for the confession of our God, if God might perhaps look kindly on us and give us an outcome like the Maccabees, as is our hope and prayer.

|But if, ignorant of this doctrine that we teach concerning the lawful defense of the lesser magistrate against the higher magistrate when this higher magistrate is attempting to wipe out the Gospel and the true church, the common people at some point abuse it and pursue a greater slaughter and destruction of the enemy than is right, this should not be counted against the Gospel or against us later on. For as we always did before, so also even now, we wanted to keep this teaching quiet, despite its being true. But overcome by the present injustice and tyranny committed by some against us, we determined that the preservation of the Gospel and the true church must be put above the possibility of such dangers from such people.

Therefore, we again affirm that God's Word is sure on this point: when the higher magistrates try to force papistic idolatry on our constitutions and oppress the true worship of God and the true worshipers themselves, as they have now begun to do, and this with no due process according to their own laws (even if they pretend differently), then faithful lesser magistrates not only can but also must resist them and defend and protect with all their power the true doctrine and worship of God, as well as the life, virtue, and possessions of their people against such tyranny.

As a defense of this true teaching, passing over many other explanations, we will now recite only these three especially clear and firm foundations.

The First Argument: From the Definition of the Terms Involved

The office of magistrate is the ordinance of God, instituted for the purpose of praising good work and punishing evil work (Romans 13[:3–4]). Therefore, when the magistrate begins to serve as a terror to good work and for the praise of evil, what he is doing is no longer the ordinance of God but the ordinance of the devil. And whoever resists such a work resists not God's ordinance but the devil's. But he who resists must resist within his own station, according to his vocation.

|The vocation closest to this task is that of another magistrate, whether a higher magistrate, or a magistrate equal in authority to the magistrate who is doing the wrong, or a lesser magistrate who is suffering the wrong. For the lesser magistrate is also himself an ordinance of God through the higher magistrate and so is obligated to serve for the praise of good and the terror of evil, in defense of his own citizens, according to God's commandment. As the higher magistrate cannot change this ordinance and command of God in his own case, so neither can he change it in another's and give license to persecuting good and promoting evil, no more than he can make the Law of God and the law of nature unjust.

So also when he removes from office a lesser magistrate who is unwilling to obey him in such a crime and replaces him with one who is willing, he is no longer an ordinance of God but an ordinance of the devil, because now he is praising and promoting evil while disgracing and destroying the good. This makes his removal of the good magistrate invalid in God's judgment, and although he has been removed, he still remains obligated to God to fulfill the office of magistrate among his people, that is, to promote the good and condemn the evil in whoever deserves it, including the higher magistrate, since Paul speaks in this passage without restriction, excepting nobody. In fact, he assigns to the higher magistrate turned tyrant the role of the devil's ordinance.

But if among the lesser magistrates most, especially those of higher rank, also themselves neglect their duty in this matter, they are committing a great crime by this negligence alone. Nor does their wicked example either excuse or obligate other lesser magistrates, though of lower rank and fewer in number. Instead, each individually ought to persevere in performing the office of magistrate according to his station and in what way he can.

Here we should also distinguish between different levels of crimes or injustices. Since there is a great distinction between them, we should consider which injustices can and ought to be resisted and in what way this should be done. We do not want to imagine that we should respond to just any form of injustice and thereby give rise to even greater disturbances.

First, then, all men, and especially magistrates, have their own vices and sins by reason of natural weakness, and so sometimes either ignorantly or carelessly commit injustices that are not overly severe or irremediable.

|In such cases, we do not at all want lesser magistrates to exercise their office against their superiors with the sword, either to punish or to defend. They can exercise their office here by serious warnings and in other civil ways. Indeed, this is what they must do. If they cannot avoid suffering injustices in this way, they should tolerate what they can tolerate without sin, and in no circumstance should they take up arms.

To this the words of 1 Peter 2:[18] properly apply: "Servants, be subject to your masters with all fear, not only to the good and kind but also to the harsh," etc. Here what is written in Exodus 22:[28] should have broad application: "Do not speak evil of a prince of your people." And with that respect and kindness[13] which Shem and Japheth showed their father, so also we should cover the shame of our higher magistrates rather than exposing it, even if this means suffering some injury ourselves.[14]

There is a second level of severe and wicked injustices, as when a prince attempts to rob a state, or an emperor wants to rob an individual prince, undeservedly and with unrighteous violence against oath and laws, either of life or of wife or of children or of privileges and authority received by inheritance or right. In such a case, though we will not say that someone is obligated by God's command to assert his right, we will say that no one who himself also holds a magistracy should be terrified by God's command from using his right as a magistrate to put up a necessary defense. Yet also here we will hope that

13 Greek: ἐπιείκεια (cf. Philippians 4:5).

14 See Genesis 9:20–23.

Christian magistrates are more ready to suffer even injuries of this sort and to leave vengeance to God, if the injustice extends only to them or only to a few and can be tolerated without sin.

Here we need to set forth the third level of injustice a magistrate can commit. This is an injustice by which the lesser magistrate is so forced to obvious sin that he cannot allow it without sinning himself, cannot omit some sort of defense, since he bears the sword for precisely this reason. Examples include when Pharaoh commands the midwives to kill the boys born to the Hebrews[15] or if he should command Moses to help in the persecution of the Israelites.[16] But here there is need of careful and true wisdom, so that no higher laws are violated in warding off the injustice, which would make this warding off of injustice also the committing of injustices, which in turn would require suppression.

In these last two levels of injustice, the magistrates who are authors of such injustices properly become and are called tyrants.

The fourth and highest level of injustice committed by higher magistrates is more than tyrannical. This happens when tyrants rise to such insanity that they persecute with deceit and arms not only the righteous persons of the lesser magistrates and their subjects but also their right itself, especially a right of so high a kind, and so highly necessary a kind, so that in persecuting their persons they are persecuting God as the Author of this right. And this not with some sudden rage that vanishes as soon as the atrocity is committed, but with the deliberate and lasting attempt to destroy a good work for all posterity.

If anyone rises to so great a height of madness, even the highest monarch, even if he does not know what he is doing, he is not only the bear-wolf, to which Luther compares the tyrant in his disputation on this matter,[17] but is the very devil himself, who can commit no crime greater or more wicked than this, except that he does it knowingly.

---

15 See Exodus 1:15–22.

16 A hypothetical, but cf. Exodus 5:4.

17 The *Circular Disputation on the Right of Resistance against the Emperor,* held on May 9, 1539 (AE 72, forthcoming). Luther refers to the pope as a "beast" and a "bear-wolf," "a monster of such a kind that cannot be called a magistrate" (WA 39/2:60). This is not simply name calling, but the biblical depiction of a wolf or bear going after the life of the sheep, that is, a false teacher who uses force in attempting to rob Christians of their souls (1 Samuel 17:34; John 10:12).

And this is the very essence, the formal cause or lifeblood, of governance in the kingdom of the devil.

And in this his governing, since his consuming desire is to extinguish every kind of divine knowledge, laws, and promises, the devil chooses for himself from among all the human race instruments suited to the task. Some serve the devil by upending and corrupting one area of knowledge; others, by upending and corrupting another. But in particular he constantly aims to extinguish the highest and chief area of divine knowledge, namely, that which concerns the true worship of God and the salvation of the human race, and the true worshipers themselves, that is, the true church of God. For this purpose, he especially incites the highest magistrates within both church and state. As it was in the time of the prophets, it was in the time of Christ and the apostles, and so it is also in our day.

If a prince or an emperor were to offend only in the realm of natural knowledge, which governs basic society and respectability in the civil sphere; if he were to proceed to such a height of insanity as to abolish the law concerning marriage and every form of chastity, and if he were to put in their place a law favoring fornication,[18] incest, and the prostitution of everyone's wives and daughters; and if he were to defend and insist on this law with might of arms so that the death penalty was set forth as punishment for all who resist or disagree—in such a case it is very obvious, and no sane person would deny it, what God's Law and command require. Namely, that such a prince or monarch, if he tries to carry out so nefarious a design, must be resisted by everyone, even by the lowest and weakest magistrates, with all the power they possess. And if this is true, how can anyone doubt, unless he is a total atheist[19] or Epicurean or Sadducee,[20] that the same resistance is just and necessary when it comes to the highest level of divine laws and knowledge, which are so integral to God's glory and every man's eternal salvation? For the glory of God cannot

---

18 *vaga libido*, the technical term for sex outside of marriage for gain, especially prostitution.

19 Greek: ἄθεος.

20 Both the Gospels and Acts depict the Sadducees, especially the chief priests, as cynical, political opportunists. See especially Caiaphas's words in John 11:50 (ESV): "Nor do you understand that it is better for you that one man should die for the people, not that the whole nation should perish." See also the plan to assassinate Paul in Acts 25:1–3.

remain among men, nor can any man's eternal salvation stand, if these laws and knowledge are lacking.

But this is exactly what our highest magistrates are doing! They are trying to abolish the true knowledge of God for all posterity, among us and everywhere else. This despite the fact that without this knowledge God cannot be truly worshiped and no mortal can be saved. More than this, they intend to justify their actions and to plant false and blasphemous opinions about God in everyone's heart and to establish the sole reign of the Antichrist and Satan in opposition to Christ. This is clearer than day, evident from the events themselves. If any doubt the reality of the situation, it can be shown by the following fact alone. Recently, certain men received an answer from a high-ranking ambassador to the effect that Caesar cannot and will not, without perjuring himself, concede anything to anyone, not even to his own brother,[21] concerning the public decree to the states of the empire made in the Augsburg Interim.[22]

From this answer, as well as from many other testimonies and circumstances, anyone can understand what we and others should expect in the end, seeing as we intend to persevere in the true religion, which is the chief reason why we have been proscribed and no reconciliation has been reached with his Majesty, the emperor.

|Based on all the foregoing explanation, I leave it to any pious and sane person to contemplate what our magistrate must do in the present perilous situation—indeed, what all pious magistrates should do, however low in rank they are. Think also what those called to fight in this battle, on either side of the fight, should do. Think what they are attacking, whom they are attacking, and with what conscience and expectation of divine judgment they are attacking them or will attack them in the future.

Our first argument has been taken from the clear Word of God, from absolutely unchangeable natural principles, and from the witness of the events themselves. It is, therefore, our chief argument

21 I.e., Ferdinand.

22 By the terms of the Augsburg Interim, Lutheran faith and Lutheran worship would be totally extinguished, with the exception of Communion in both kinds and the marriage of priests. See Augsburg Interim, Preface: "With the exception of two articles on communion under both kinds and marriage of priests, it does not vary from our true [Roman] Catholic religion and ecclesiastical doctrines, statutes, and ordinances" (*SC*, 147).

in this disputation, true and irrefutable. As explained, this argument exposes the spectacle of the incalculably horrific crime committed by our enemies. In turn, it commends the just cause and the godly zeal of those who are making a defense. It also sets great and eternal rewards before them, together with an outcome worthy of those zealous for the Law of our God.

The Second Argument

Christ commands positively in regard to both Caesar and God that what belongs to Caesar be rendered to Caesar and what belongs to God be rendered to God.[23] We therefore rightly infer the negative from this positive statement, and this as regards both Caesar and God. So also the commandments, as is the case with the Ten Commandments, are stated in the negative but include a positive meaning.

Therefore and first, according to the meaning of Jesus' command here, what belongs to God must not be rendered to Caesar. The apostles also hand down this precept and rule: "We must obey God rather than man."[24] Denying obedience to superiors in those things which are promoted against God is not to deny their authority, nor can those who do so be counted contentious or rebellious, as Daniel says, "I have done nothing wrong against you, O king."[25]

There are two reasons why they cannot be accused of committing this crime. First, since those now holding the office of magistrate are demanding this obedience not as magistrates according to the ordinance of God but as mere men, that is, as those who have no higher authority in this matter according to the Word of God. This appears to be the explanation the apostles intended to make by their statement. Then again, even if they remained true magistrates, still, as in human rankings of power the law of a higher magistrate overrides the law of a lower magistrate, so divine laws necessarily override human laws.[26]

23 Matthew 22:21.

24 Acts 5:29.

25 Daniel 6:22.

26 Luther makes the same argument in *Circular Disputation on the Right of Resistance against the Emperor*: "A lesser law must always give way to a higher law. The First Table of the Law is higher than the Second" (WA 39/2:70 [cf. AE 72]).

Second, just as Christ does not want what belongs to God attributed to Caesar, neither does He want what belongs to others attributed to Caesar, when they simply are not his according to either divine or even imperial law. So if contrary to divine laws Caesar should demand my life or someone else's life, or the chastity of my wife or my daughter, or my possessions, etc., I ought not hand these over to him. So Naboth was unwilling to sell his vineyard to Ahab, even when Ahab asked for it and offered him money for it.[27] Ambrose also refused to give the cathedral over to the Arians despite the Empress Justina's command to do so.[28] Lawrence refused to hand over the treasury of the church to Decius.[29] Would that both princes and subjects thought on this [divine] Law and these examples often, wherever and whenever necessary.

Third, since Christ connects everything together in His command that what belongs to Caesar be rendered to Caesar and what belongs to God be rendered to God and what belongs to individuals be rendered to individuals, when Caesar demands what belongs to him or what is owed to him in such a way that he is thereby necessarily also claiming for himself things that belong to God or others, and these things cannot be given him without committing sin, then the interconnectedness of Christ's command means that in this case we would also have to refuse Caesar the things which were his or which were owed to him.

Let us look at the example of a head of household. If he comes home to his wife and adolescent daughters accompanied by charlatans and with the obvious intention of prostituting them, then they, his wife and daughters, not only should not admit their husband and father, an obedience they would otherwise owe him, but they should also drive him back with stones, since they cannot otherwise preserve their chastity.

---

27 See 1 Kings 21:1–16.

28 Cassiodorus (ca. 485–ca. 580), *Tripartite History* IX. Justina was the mother of the sitting emperor, Valentinian II (r. 375–392). The Arians denied the divinity of Christ. Their teachings were condemned at the Council of Nicaea in 325. Ambrose famously said, "What belongs to God is outside the emperor's power" (Letter 20.19 [cf. NPNF² 10:425]).

29 St. Lawrence, when commanded to hand the treasure of the church over to the emperor, famously pointed to the Christian poor and said, "Here is the church's treasure." Cf. Jacobus de Voragine, *The Golden Legend*, ch. 117, "On St. Lawrence, Martyr."

In the same way, when the entrance of Caesar into a city brings with it the abolition of the true religion and the slaughter and exile of the faithful believers, in such a case the defense of the city, its life, and the innocent people within it (which defense the magistrates of this city owe to God according to God's own command) withholds that part of the obedience normally owed to Caesar, lest such obedience allow him into the city. | And this according to the rule of Christ, which states that when the duties we normally owe someone entail sin and injury to God and others, they should be paid to no one, not even to a father or magistrate.

Fourth, on the basis of this same passage—"Render to Caesar the things that belong to Caesar and to God the things that belong to God"—while Christ is indeed putting other men under Caesar's authority, He is at the same time putting them and Caesar himself under God's authority. He wants the highest authority among men (such as Caesar's authority) to serve God in particular, so that Caesar is to take care that both he himself and those subject to his power render to God what belongs to God according to God's Word, and that those who act to the contrary be restrained. This, in fact, belongs properly and principally to the office of a Christian magistrate, as even this passage shows to some extent and as we have demonstrated elsewhere more clearly from other testimonies, arguments, and examples from God's Word.

Therefore, when the highest prince not only himself refuses to render to God what belongs to God but also robs this divine honor from others, using his authority as a pretext for his actions, even asserting his authority with the sword, there still remains among men an authority ordained by God: the authority to defend God's honor.

Indeed, at the death of an emperor, the other princes and states who were under him individually exercise in their own vicinity whatever power of his that is temporarily transferred to them (and they ought to exercise this power because of God's command), which includes the restraining of blasphemers and of those who are by threat of the sword forcing others to blaspheme. It includes also using the sword themselves to keep the aggressors from the necks of their citizens. Therefore, according to the same authority, they ought to keep the sitting highest magistrate from doing the same outside of and contrary to his office, since he is acting, I say, by the ordinance of the devil, not by the ordinance of God, as was shown above from Paul.

To this also pertains the psalm: "I said, 'You are gods,' but you will die like men."[30] That is: "When you abandon My ordinance whereby I put you in authority over other men, so that you would act in My stead among them by rewarding the good and punishing the evil, and instead you serve what is shameful, acting just as other wicked men, then I will have no regard for your majesty or your authority. | You will be punished the same as the rest, both by Me and by others to whom I will give this authority of punishing and restraining wicked men, each one according to his vocation."

The Third Argument

If God intends higher magistrates to be completely inviolable by virtue of His ordinance and command, even after they become tyrants, how many godless and absurd results would follow? In particular, it would follow that God, by His own ordinance and command, was fortifying—no, more than that—was honoring and helping evil, and that He was impeding the good—no, more than that—was destroying the good! Thus it would follow that there are contrary intentions in the nature of God Himself and in His institution of the ordinance of magistrate, that by this ordinance God was oppressing the human race no less than He was advancing it.

This is all quite obvious, and no sane person can deny it. If by His ordinance and command God concedes such impunity even to the greatest tyrant, who will remain innocent before God in trying, if he can, to prevent such a man from destroying the whole earth? Who will not also, when the tyrant demands it, provide his property, as well as the bodies under his care, and finally his life itself, all to advance the causes, objects, and promotion of tyranny, and this in accordance with God's command? Who will do what is right against the tyrant's will and survive it? Will there be even one man left among all who does the right thing? Therefore, God intends and at the same time does not intend evil! He casts down and raises up evil among magistrates, by His own ordinance!

And since no proclivity is more common to man than to abuse the authority and impunity granted by God for good, and use that very authority for evil; since nothing is easier for the devil than to

30 Psalm 82:6–7.

incite such a man and change him from a man into a devil; and since nothing could be more desirable to the devil and more advantageous for strengthening his kingdom (which is the kingdom of sin and death) than to effectually bind the consciences of men with the sure Word and command of God, so that they dare not hinder him from doing his wicked work through the magistrate ordained by God, it very clearly follows from all this that when the highest magistrate is reduced to insane raging, |God by His very own ordinance and command has overturned that which is good in the ordinance of magistrate and has betrayed His very own laws instead of promoting them and has exposed righteous men to the fury of tyrants and the devil.

Therefore, it is an abominable noise that Satan prattles concerning the authority of the Roman pope: that to him belongs such impunity, so that, even if he knowingly led infinite souls to hell, still no one could say to him, "What are you doing?" No one could resist him.[31] By this horrible lie he has strengthened the tyranny of his Antichrist beyond measure. So now also we understand the real reasons why this persuasion concerning the impunity of the highest ruler or of higher magistrates is not only senseless but also has been invented by the devil at this time for the express purpose of destroying the remnant of Christ's kingdom and restoring the kingdom of the Antichrist and the devil.

We know that God Himself has repressed and still can repress tyrannical persecutors of the Gospel and the church, and that the kingdom of Christ can neither be established nor defended nor preserved by the sword,[32] but this does not stand opposed to our reasoning and judgment in this matter.

|God has always punished evil men, tyrants in particular. At times He does so without the service of men, in ways of His own, whether hidden or manifest. But at times He does it through men. Sometimes He even punishes evil men through evil men. But ordinarily He does it through those men who are carrying out a righteous defense according to their calling. As it is said about those guilty of murder: "By man shall his blood be shed" (Genesis 9:[6]).

---

31 *Decretum Gratiani*, Part I, D. 40, c. 6, states that even if the pope is wicked and is leading innumerable people astray to hell, "no one among mortals presumes to condemn his faults, because he who is to judge all ought himself be judged by no one, unless he is found to have strayed from the faith."

32 Cf. John 18:36 (ESV): "My kingdom is not of this world."

This duty of carrying out defense or of fending off unjust violence is the divine and proper office of the magistrate, whether of a higher magistrate against a lower magistrate, or of a magistrate against another of equal rank, or of a lower magistrate against a higher magistrate. For God has communicated this His office to all legitimate magistrates and not only to one rank or to one person. He has given it for the defense and praise of good and not of evil, for the whole course of this life, not only at one time or another. For Paul speaks without restriction when he defines the office of magistrate, excepting no rank, no person, no evil, no time, where good men should not be defended by the office of every magistrate, even one of the lowest rank.

If exception is made for the higher magistrates and the sins by which they seek to extinguish natural law and religion, it would be necessary to find this exception taught in the express Word of God, but no one will ever show such a thing to us. Yet we can show even further that God is no respecter of persons[33] and so does not give anyone impunity by His Word and ordinance, especially for crimes of the greatest magnitude. On the contrary, in His very institution of magistrates, He very strictly prohibits respect of persons[34] in passing judgment. Moses and Jehoshaphat say it: "The judgment you administer is God's judgment."[35] Therefore, when a magistrate restrains a tyrant, it is clear that the same tyrant has been restrained by God.

|What an absurdity it would be if God had instituted the ordinance of magistrate, so holy and necessary for the human race, in such a way that one man, in whose hands was all the power, having gone mad, could almost completely destroy this ordinance or turn it into its opposite, according to his own will! And then when other men were able and willing to preserve this ordinance in an orderly way and without confusion, God would not allow it to them!

Finally, as to establishing and defending the kingdom of Christ, we respond very simply and truly that this cannot be done by any human plans, arms, or other humanly devised ways. Yet just as the works of a godly magistrate can and ought, according to the ordinance and command of God, serve the kingdom of Christ by regulating and

33 Greek: προσωποληπτήν. Cf. Acts 10:34; Romans 2:11; Ephesians 6:9; Colossians 3:25.

34 Greek: προσωποληψίαν.

35 See Deuteronomy 1:17; 2 Chronicles 19:6.

providing for the ministry of Word and Sacraments, so also his arms should serve in defending this same ministry and the entire church against unjust persecution.

These are very strong reasons for approving the necessary defense of a lower magistrate against a higher magistrate in the present persecution of the Gospel. They are also powerful enough to fortify the consciences of all pious and good men, so that everyone may know what he should do when called on either to bear arms against the Gospel of Christ or to repel an attack against this Gospel.

Other arguments supporting this position, including those which are found throughout the Roman legal code, can be found in the writings of the best theologians before our time, as well as from the writings of those who agreed with us in the assertion of godly defense before this present persecution arose against us. We have not changed our position in any way, nor are we saying anything new, just as we have remained consistent in the other articles of the pure doctrine. This is also the position of the man of God, Luther, set forth in several passages and letters and also defended in a public disputation well before this war broke out.[36]

The reason why, in some other writings, the same Luther frequently argued ambiguously concerning this same subject, he himself explained privately to some and clarifies quite publicly in the book published as *Against the Assassin at Dresden*.[37] There he says that he wanted to restrain both sides. He did not at that time wish to say that a defense was completely unlawful, lest he thereby arm the Papists. But he also did not want, by his praise or approval of the right of defense, to make good men unwilling to endure less offensive injuries imposed by the enemy and so to further excite the already crazed Thrasos,[38] who he knew wanted war anyway, so stupid and thoroughly carnal

36 The public disputation mentioned is *Circular Disputation on the Right of Resistance against the Emperor* (1539), WA 39/2:39–91 (AE 72).

37 A pamphlet written in 1531, *Against the Assassin at Dresden*, was one of a series of pamphlets Luther wrote attacking the Roman Catholic Duke George of Saxony (WA 30/3:446–71). It is an especially spirited polemic against Roman Catholic theology.

38 Thraso is the name of an overly aggressive soldier in Terence's comedy *The Eunuch*. The name itself means "bold."

were their desires. Luther makes the most serious complaints about such men in his commentary on Psalm 118.[39]

We would certainly want to do the same thing if matters today were unchanged from what they were then. Now only a small remnant of the faithful remains. To destroy this remnant, in a diabolical mockery of Christ and His Word, the Papists are even arming those who, against their conscience, departed from us. Nor do they desire simply that this miserable remnant be destroyed, but that the very doctrine and glory of Christ which is among us be eradicated and the abominations of the Antichrist be established forever. Since these things are so, in line with the clear explanation of the true teaching concerning defense, we are forced to consider this obvious overthrow of Christ, the Gospel, and the church of far greater consequence than whatever punishments our persecutors may impose—of far greater consequence, in fact, than the entire world.

Finally, if anyone wants to see examples of lower magistrates putting up a defense against higher magistrates, he will find many relevant cases if he studies the events recorded in biblical, ecclesiastical, and pagan history.

The history of the Maccabees fits well here (1 Maccabees 2). Although they had been conquered and were already under the rule of King Antiochus, they resisted him when he declared his intention to impose the same religion on all nations and was trying to force the people of God to worship idols. They made an armed defense of both their own lives and the Law or worship of God, as is expressly written in that book.

Jehu, one of the princes under King Joram, takes up arms against his king to mete out punishment on him and the entire house of Ahab because of the persecution they perpetrated against the true worship of God and the faithful (2 Kings 9). And although he did this at the special direction of God and he does some unique and inimitable things, still God also wanted by this example to illustrate the common calling of faithful magistrates, namely, that they must oppose higher magistrates who are persecuting true worship and the true church.

---

39 Written in 1530, Luther comments that since so many evil men abound in the world, we should "thank God for temporal peace, authority, and government" (AE 14:41–106, here at p. 52).

The people of God, finding serious fault with King Saul, free his son Jonathan from the hand of his father, who desired to kill him on the basis of superstition. They defended him by force, or they were at least prepared to defend him by force, and this not unjustly. For they say, "As the Lord lives, not a hair from his head will fall to the earth, since he has worked with God today" (1 Samuel 14:[45]).

Then there is the example of Asa, who removed his mother from office and destroyed her idols (1 Kings 15:[13]). When diligently considered, this example lends not a little clarity and weight to this argument.

Similar to this is the example of Ambrose, who used his authority as bishop to condemn the Emperor Theodosius and keep Theodosius from entering the cathedral because of the slaughter he had perpetrated on the people of Thessalonica.[40]

The Armenians, once they became Christians, defended themselves with arms against the edicts of Emperor Maximinus, who tried to force them to exchange the Christian religion for the worship of idols.[41] Likewise, it was for the defense of the Christians that Emperor Constantine took up arms against Licinius, his fellow ruler over the empire.[42]

The most praiseworthy and powerful Emperor Trajan spoke from the sanctuary of natural law itself when he addressed the question of lower magistrates putting up a defense against higher magistrates, and this even in political matters. When he appointed a Master of the Horse for himself, he handed him a sword and said, "Use this sword

40 Cassiodorus, *Tripartite History* IX. Around AD 390, after Theodosius (r. 379–395) ordered the massacre of a large number of Thessalonian citizens, Ambrose, bishop of Milan, called him to repentance and refused him the Sacrament. Theodosius submitted to Ambrose and repented.

41 Eusebius (ca. 263–339), *Church History* IX.8. Emperor Maximinus II (r. 310–313) followed the policy of Diocletian (r. 284–305) in the eastern Roman Empire and ruthlessly persecuted Christians. His special attention was on the frontier nation of Armenia. It was Constantine who, after his victory over Maxentius at the Milvian Bridge (AD 312), ordered Maximinus II to cease persecution of the Armenian Christians.

42 Eusebius, *Church History* X.9. While it had long been the custom to have more than one emperor over the vast Roman Empire, Constantine took sole rule over the empire after his defeat of Licinius in AD 324. Despite jointly issuing the Edict of Milan in AD 313 with Constantine, which decriminalized Christianity, Licinius soon grew jealous of Christian support of Constantine and began persecuting Christians in defiance of the edict.

against my enemies if I command what is just. But if I command what is unjust, use it against me."[43] This saying is famous and truly belongs to natural, that is, divine Law. Therefore, just as Christ in the Gospel does not abolish other knowledge of principles, whether theoretical or practical, or the Law of God itself, but rather establishes it (as the apostle says),[44] so neither does He abolish this teaching concerning necessary defense. Indeed, Christian magistrates can faithfully employ it. No, because of God's command, they are obligated to employ it. This we have now shown fully enough with testimonies, proofs, and examples taken from the Word of God.

If anyone thinks we have been too harsh in explaining these things, let him consider that Christ suffers far more harshly in this persecution and that He demands of us that we testify to the truth. |That being said, we have tempered our style quite a bit, and the observant and fair reader will easily notice that we have only wanted to speak the facts themselves and to spare people as much as we could. If we do not obtain peace, we can intensify what we have said here and add many things in addition. We would do so truly and seriously and as our office demands, even if the same reward awaits us in this world as the prophets, John the Baptist, Christ, the apostles, and many others like them, who suffered for acting as we are now.

43 Recorded in Cassius Dio (ca. 150–325), [*Roman History,*] 68.5.

44 Romans 3:31 (ESV): "Do we then overthrow the law by this faith? By no means! On the contrary, we uphold the law."

THE THIRD PART OF THIS LITTLE BOOK

Or, an Exhortation

FROM what we have written above in our confession and apology, the observant reader already understands not what we are asking, but what God is demanding from each one of us, both from those who are outside our walls and from all of us in this city and church. This can and should, on the one hand, terrify men from bringing unjust violence against us. On the other hand, it should also encourage men to repel this unjust violence. Nevertheless, to place these duties and the reasons for them in plain sight, we will briefly set forth in this epilogue the main points.

First, it is clear that no godly or Christian man can aid our enemies against us either by fighting for them or by offering them advice, money, or other supplies. The only reason why our city cannot obtain peace is because we always make specific mention of the Gospel in any condition of peace, insisting that we cannot change it or diminish it in the least; and the enemy clearly manifests its intention to oppress this entire teaching of Christ and to restore the Antichrist in any way they can. How, then, I ask, can it be denied any longer that we are not being targeted in this war chiefly for political reasons, concerning which our side would happily come to an agreement, but that the chief targets (never mind us!) are Christ Himself and His Word? But we are unwilling to lose this Word or to accept the abominations of the Antichrist.

Whether you are a magistrate or a subject, if you are in any way involved in this war or in the execution of the proscription against us, consider to what cause you are devoting your advice, your money, your works, your body, your very life and soul. And to whom are you allying yourself? Is it not to the enemies of Christ and His Word? Are you not cooperating in the very work whereby they desire to erase the knowledge and glory of Christ not only from their territories but also from all the world and to put their papistic idolatry and blasphemies in its place? The work by which they persecute Christ in His members with thoroughly satanic fury, stain their hands in Christ's blood, and trample Him under their feet?

Nor will anyone be excused before God on the grounds that he does not know what is being done. Those who once crucified Christ did not know that He was the Son of God, but were not therefore excused. For they should have known it from Christ's sermons and miracles, just as all today should know the public matters that have to do with the glory of Christ and their own salvation. So that no one can ignore these matters, we are now making them public to all. If anyone is still ignorant of them after this, let him be ignorant, and he will be ignored. For it is insolent to willfully ignore a thing that is already clear in itself and has now been explained by many.

Affected ignorance in no way excuses these men from blame. They are still persecutors of Christ. Much less will the claim of others that their decision was forced from them hold as an excuse. A decision, even if forced, is still a decision and therefore will reap the rewards due to persecutors. It is worse than ignorance. This is now the state of things among so many who until now had confessed the Gospel with us. If it were possible for some powerful leader in our time to hand over Christ, the Son of God, to be put to death in the flesh, he would have many Christians obey his decree, if he gave the choice between punishment or death on the one hand and life or rewards of honor and riches on the other. Some, captivated by the pleasantness of this life, of rewards and honors; some, persuaded for other reasons (provided that they saw Christ the Son of God set before them weak and abandoned by God), would again crucify the Lord according to the will of the tyrant.

But how is this different from what is being committed against us? For Christ Himself gives this testimony: "Whatever you do to one of the least of these, you have done the same to Me."[1] And to Saul He says, "Saul, Saul, why are you persecuting Me?"[2]

1 Matthew 25:40.

2 Acts 9:4.

For this reason, we no longer wonder so much at the wickedness and cruelty of the Jews against Christ, since we now see things reminiscent of the whole history of His Passion and death in the persons and actions of many disciples of the Gospel (such were some up till now, or at least want to seem to have been). We see this with the deepest grief. And we will soon see this even more.

There are now not only those who are like the apostles at the crucifixion of the Lord, grieving, silent, fleeing, and denying. There are also those like Judas. There are others who suddenly go from the happy greeting of "Hosanna!" on Palm Sunday to the fatal and bloodthirsty cry, "Away with Him. Away with Him! Crucify Him! Crucify Him!"[3] There are those carrying out their wicked plans, employing taunts, hands, whipping, plundering, and everything else that precedes the crucifixion itself.[4]

But how did so sudden a change come on the disciples of the Gospel? It is surely the result of their departing from the Word. This departure, first perpetrated among the heads of states, and that against conscience, soon crept down into the other members of the body.

In fact, in the latest convention at Augsburg, our princes and states abandoned the Word and promised that they and their subjects would obey first the council and then the Interim.[5] And now, without repentance, some are seeking excuses, escapes, even justifications for their faithlessness. But the emperor is demanding that they keep their promise and is now using his authority to command us to be attacked. Soon he will command also all the others who do not acquiesce completely to the Interim or the papacy to be attacked and slaughtered.

Thus because few perhaps, or none at all, will want to retract the faithless promise they made to the emperor, or to suffer anything because of it, they will knowingly become crucifiers of Christ Himself in the persons of all His faithful. So this faithlessness, whereby men knowingly depart from the Word in matters of doctrine, grows with horrific increase.

---

3 Cf. John 12:13; 19:15.

4 Cf. John 19:1–3; Luke 22:63–65.

5 This promise is in the very text of the Augsburg Interim, both in the Preface, which states: "They should join in consenting to adhere to and submit to this council [of Trent]"; and in Article XI, "On the Authority and Power of the Church," which confesses that the decisions of councils are binding on the whole church (*SC*, 146, 157–58).

But a still greater punishment is the apathy with which so many can dismiss so great a crime. Even more, they excuse it, praise it, glory in their wickedness. Indeed, this apathy is the first punishment imposed on the sin against the Holy Spirit. But now they are adding to their conscious rejection of the truth also the persecution of the same truth. This sin against the Holy Spirit has certainly already been committed by very many.

Christ says that this sin is unforgivable, not because it cannot be forgiven to those who repent but because such men never do repent, since God has departed from them.[6] To them it happens as the psalm says, "He loved cursing, and so it will come on him. He refused to bless, and so blessing will depart far from him."[7] Thus they either turn into open despisers of God or become self-secure, like the priests and Pharisees. Or else they despair like Cain and Judas when they feel the wrath of God upon them. These times will soon provide many horrible examples of such men. If any, with Peter, knowingly deny Jesus through weakness or, with Paul, ignorantly persecute Him, we pray for them that God give them repentance like Peter and Paul.

But we encourage every individual to carefully consider this distinction between persecutors. There are those who knowingly persecute what they know to be true. These have committed the sin against the Holy Spirit, and none has ever come to repentance, according to Christ's Word. Then there are others who ignorantly persecuted what they did not know. But how many of these are found to have been converted?

And I really do not know which is the greater crime: to not know that the doctrine you are persecuting is true, as Paul did not know when he was persecuting Christians, or to unknowingly persecute, along with open persecutors, what you yourself hold to be the doctrine of Christ. Although the emperor has said that he is not persecuting us because of our doctrine but because of our rebellion or because of some other sins, yet everyone among the Evangelicals[8] serving as soldiers under him cannot but know that the emperor is simultaneously and especially persecuting in us this religion, since the rebellion of which he accuses us has arisen because of the necessary defense

6 Matthew 12:31–32.

7 Psalm 109:17.

8 "Evangelical" was the normal term for "Lutheran."

of this religion. |Therefore, those pseudo-Evangelicals who aid the emperor with advice, oaths, money, or arms against us have become persecutors of what they know is true, whether or not they know that they are committing so great a crime, or willfully do not want to know.

And those who die in this beginning of the war or those who will die in further conflicts, will they not die as persecutors of Christ? How can they possibly hope for forgiveness from the very One whom they are persecuting? Or how will they be able to deny what they have done or excuse the fact that they persecuted Christ in this war? Their very own conscience will then accuse them, since the conscience puts off hypocrisy and ignorance at such a time and stands naked and alone before the judgment seat of God, forced to acknowledge the truth of what has happened.

But this is certainly the great mark of God's anger and His impending righteous judgment, and at the same time the mark of the extreme fury of the devil against Christ, that Christian men are now compelled to an armed persecution of their own religion, the true religion. And this when heathen do not hesitate to take up arms to protect their false religion! There has truly been nothing like this in any history of any time, in the church or among the heathen, since the beginning of the world.

Therefore, this sin will present the most horrendous spectacle of all to God, angels, men, and the whole creation at God's final judgment. It will carry with it the most hideous punishments imaginable, suffered together with the demons. If some have this revealed to their conscience during this life, since God doubtless will make some men examples and signs of His vengeance, they will find their comfort and reward with Judas and will hasten to receive the payment due their deeds in eternal death.[9]

No matter how harshly this has been spoken, it has still not been spoken harshly enough, nor can it be spoken or conceived harshly enough, to equal the magnitude of the sin and God's wrath against it. Nor are we now setting these things before the world with a thought only of saving our lives or out of great anxiety for them. Although we acknowledge our weakness, we overcome our flesh by faith and consider how by the very loss of this life we can carry off the reward and crown of martyrdom. Therefore, the primary reason for publishing

9 Cf. Matthew 27:3–5; Acts 1:16–19.

this work is that we must fight for the Gospel of Jesus Christ against Satan and his ministers, not only by refuting his lies but also by impeding his slaughters, since it is by both of these tactics that he is now so violently assaulting the true religion.

Finally, we ought to have the greatest regard for the little children and for all posterity who will meet no little obstacle to their eternal salvation if we here and other faithful men elsewhere are all slaughtered by Satan and the godless world.

Let the wise of the world and the Epicureans laugh at this, until that time when their laughing turns to lamentation. Let the tyrants rage the more, so that they more quickly fill up their measure. Even if, according to God's will, we ourselves cannot be kept alive, we still look to save those good and decent people outside our walls, to keep them safe from wicked persecution, and to leave to our posterity a seed of the Word that brings eternal life.

Now we address those who are our brothers in Christ Jesus. We have no doubt that among all the churches, even those currently oppressed by tyranny, there remain many who do not want the purity of the Evangelical doctrine to be oppressed or the idolatries of the papacy to be restored; who want even less to become themselves persecutors of the Gospel and of Christ, or aiders and abettors to the Antichrist, thus burdening themselves with the sins of his whole anti-Christian kingdom; who do not wish to disrupt this printing press,[10] which Christ has instituted in this city for the sake of the whole church during this hour of the power of darkness, in order to fight against the Antichrist with His proper weapons, that is, by the Spirit of His mouth, etc.[11]

If those who are so minded ponder these things faithfully in their minds, they will realize that now is the necessary time for them to confess Christ with both mouth and action, though they can hardly confess Him now without bringing definite danger on themselves. In my judgment, there is no one so wise in our day that he can escape all harm and danger, unless he joins definitively in the denial or persecution of Christ. If some are unwilling to believe this, they can enjoy

10 Besides publishing the Magdeburg Confession, the printing presses in Magdeburg published many other tracts against the Interimists and the Adiaphorists. See below, p. 118 n. 18.

11 Cf. 2 Thessalonians 2:8.

their dreams now, but though they are now unwilling to undergo a small and brief loss in bodily and material things, they will soon suffer a much more serious loss in their consciences and souls. Pray God it is not an eternal loss! There are even now many in our company and many elsewhere who testify personally and in their writings to the disquiet of their consciences which they willingly inflicted on themselves at the start of these compromises,[12] some because of cowardice, some in the guise of wisdom, some by silly excuses for these compromises.

|In the life of Maurice, there is the account of the Thebans.[13] When Diocletian and Maximian, emperors who were exceedingly hostile to the Christians, ordered the Thebans to take up arms to subjugate rebels against the Roman Empire, the Thebans acted in accord with Christ's command to render to God the things that are God's and to Caesar the things that are Caesar's. Uncertain who the rebels were against whom the war was being waged, they sent to the emperor a chosen legion of soldiers, with this command: they would aid the emperor in just wars, but they would by no means take up arms against Christians. They would instead defend them against unjust violence. Maurice was chosen general of this legion.

Maurice then came with his legion to the Emperor Maximian, and when his entire army had been gathered at Ottodorum, he received the orders that everyone must enter into a pact and swear an oath against the rebels of the Roman Empire, in particular, the Christians, whom Maximian condemned as rebels (as is the case now with us) simply because they refused to deny their faith in Christ and sacrifice to idols.

Then Maurice and all the faithful soldiers withdrew and sent to the emperor to say that they were doing nothing seditious in this matter, that they remained in fact the soldiers of the emperor and were ready in arms for the defense of the republic, but that they would in no way abandon their faith in Christ or act contrary to it. |The brave soldiers of Christ so persevered in this most holy decision that, as they were unable to escape the hands of the rest of the invading army, they all

12 Literally: "changes," referring to the compromises that arose from the changes in worship practice because of the Augsburg Interim and imperial pressure.

13 Jacobus de Voragine, *The Golden Legend*, ch. 141. St. Maurice served as general over the Theban legion in the Roman army during the persecutions of Diocletian and Maximian (r. 286–305).

submitted willingly to martyrdom rather than take up arms against other Christians or deny the Lord of life and Author of salvation.[14]

The guards of Saul unanimously and unitedly refused to follow the king's command to kill the priests of Nob (1 Samuel 22:[16–17]). Thus they brought on themselves the hatred of the king and the dangers that accompany that hatred. But if there were, as there certainly should be according to God's command, the same unanimity and consensus of many good men today in the refusal of military service, cooperation, and contributions for oppressing us or other faithful Christians, then even if those Sauls still had their Edomite Doegs,[15] yet at least the faithful would have had some remedy for their consciences in this matter, since it is not easy for so many to be forced to perpetrate so great an injustice at the same time. Perhaps they would escape punishment like Saul's guards.

But if they could not escape punishment, they should rather flee or suffer the persecution or, if they hold a lesser magistracy, employ their men in a proper defense against unjust violence. As shown above, this right of defense is confirmed by divine, natural, and human law. It is especially the prerogative within our German Empire, where higher and lesser magistrates are mutually bound by definite laws and privileges. Christian magistrates can use these laws and privileges rightly and with a good conscience, just as they can use other political ordinances that do not conflict with God's Word.

|Up to this point, we have spoken of one aspect of the duty of Christians, that they should keep themselves free from any persecution of the Gospel, of Christ, or of His members and from the sin against the Holy Spirit. This is their duty in this war being waged against us and precludes any participation in the execution of the proscription against us with the enemies of the Gospel and of Christ, with apostates, and with those who are knowingly ignoring their duty.

Now we come to the second aspect of the duty of faithful Christians. God gives His command concerning this in Proverbs 24:[11–12], saying, "Deliver those who are being led to death, and free those who are drawn to destruction. If you say, 'We have no strength,' He who sees the heart, He understands. Nothing

14 Maurice, along with his army of Christians, suffered a martyr's death ca. AD 286.

15 Doeg the Edomite carried out the order of Saul, killing eighty-five priests together with their wives and children (1 Samuel 22:18–19).

escapes the Keeper of your soul. He will return to a man according to his deeds."

This passage warns Christians of two things. First, that it is not enough to not join with the godless against us. It is necessary also to offer the aid we need so that we might not be oppressed unjustly. Thus the guards of Saul, though they did not lift their hands against the priests of Nob or consent to their killing, are not therefore free from the crime of the slaughter that was perpetrated because they did not help the innocent or defend them.

Second, this passage warns Christians that the excuses which they are inventing for themselves as reasons to desert us are in no way acceptable to God. They do not make them guiltless of our blood and the blood of Christ, on account of whom we are suffering this persecution.

The following are the different excuses variously alleged by one or another. First, that they cannot question their higher magistrates when they say that they are waging war not because of our religion but because of our rebellion. Second, that they lack the strength. Third, that they lack the right to help us, since we are opposing higher magistrates. There are other excuses too. God knows the emptiness of these excuses and whatever other excuses can now be thought up. He urges this emptiness on the consciences of individuals, that they cannot deceive God, that they will pay the penalty for their desertion of Him. |This passage is therefore an explanation of the Fifth Commandment, which makes guilty of murder not only those who take life unjustly but also those who do not protect their own life or others' lives against unjust violence, according to their ability.[16]

If we are true members of Christ, if we are members of one body in Christ, united and made alive by His one Spirit, then what the apostle affirms about this body of Christ will now be very obvious: "When one member suffers, all the members suffer together."[17] The members care for one another and help one another.

Therefore, those who do not share in this care and completely refuse to render service to the other suffering members, these are

16 Cf. Luther's treatment of the Fifth Commandment in LC I 191: "God also rightly calls all people murderers who do not provide counsel and help in distress and danger of body and life" (*Concordia*, 380; cf. *BoC*, 412).

17 1 Corinthians 12:26.

either not members of Christ's body at all or are dead members, or are something less than half alive. For it is impossible for living members of a living body not to be affected with the other members, not to seek to do something in their own way and their own place, not to bring help to the other hurting members.

|We should also speak of the benefits this city has rendered to the rest of the body of all Christendom. In light of these benefits, not only should this city not be forsaken, but it cannot be forsaken without inflicting great damage on the same body. This city alone has published the books that have unmasked the lies surrounding the Interim and the controversy over adiaphora.[18] Without these warnings, even the elect could have been led into error.[19] This city alone has impeded the plans and attempts of the enemy to restore the papacy and oppress the freedom of our fatherland, so that whatever is left outside our walls of the former purity of the ministry or of the former freedom of politics (which is admittedly very little), this God seems to have bestowed anew, as it were, through this His chaste virgin,[20] whom He has chosen for this purpose.

And this same virgin is expending her life and all that belongs to her for the sake of preserving the chastity and freedom of others no less than her own. What equality would there then be, if others enjoy the benefits of this city but are unwilling to take any part in its danger or misfortune, especially in so great a cause, which encompasses the glory of God and the prosperity of the whole church?

Let them remember now how severe God's judgment is against those who abandon faithful Christians, concerning which we possess a weighty and sobering history in Judges 5. There we read how the weakest two tribes of Israel, Zebulun and Naphtali, risked their lives for the worship of God and for the rest of the people in the conflict

---

18 In the years 1549 and 1550, the publishing house of Michael Lotter and other printers in Magdeburg published a massive number of tracts exposing the compromises of the Augsburg and Leipzig Interims. Publications included works by Matthias Flacius, Johann Brenz, Nicolaus von Amsdorf, Joachim Westphal, and many others. Typical of the works is Joachim Westphal, *Four Sermons on Guarding the Precious Treasure of God's Word and Sacred Worship against Their Many Thieves: The Papists, the Interimists, and the Adiaphorists* (Magdeburg: Lotter, 1550).

19 Cf. Matthew 24:24.

20 A play on the name of Magdeburg as "Mädchenburg," i.e., "Virgin City." The name was Hellenized as Parthenopolis and Latinized as Virginopolis at the time of the Reformation (*AS* 608 n. 268).

against Jabin, king of Canaan, who then held power over God's people and exercised his tyranny against them. The other three more powerful tribes, however, remained passive, perhaps awaiting the outcome of this tragedy, thinking that if the army of the enemy should come out victorious, they themselves would be in less danger, but if God gave a happy outcome to their fellow, small, and weak little tribes, they themselves would still enjoy the fruits of the victory, without having exerted any labor or undergone any danger, as the blood of their brothers was shed and many of their lives lost to certain death (as is happening in our time). |Then God, refusing to suffer such inequality to stand (we will not use harsher language here), commanded an angel to pronounce a curse on the three tribes that deserted their brothers, "because," he says, "they did not come to the help of the Lord" (Judges 5:[23]). He complains that it was not merely men, but He Himself who was abandoned by His people.

There are similar duties that should bind other faithful Christians to this city and by which they can help her, according to the saying of Solomon. These are as follows:

First, prayer. As James 5:[16] says, "Pray for one another." We do not doubt that these prayers, which arise in true faith and with such unanimity from all Christ's members, and which concern a matter so important to Christ Himself and to His church, are abundantly efficacious and have the divine power to change the outcome above and beyond the plans and powers of man. These prayers have up to this point held back Satan's fury, lest he completely obliterate the remnant of the true ministry and the true church in our Germany.

The second duty is supplication of the higher magistrates. If this supplication should happen with the combined urging of the majority of states and faithful Christians, as it should, and if it is combined with the confession of their faith and an appeal to the duty to make a necessary defense of the innocent for the sake of the common cause of Christ, His Gospel, and His entire church, there is no doubt that it would bend somewhat the proud minds of the higher magistrates and persuade them (or restrain them) toward moderation.

|If this seems to any "a hard word,"[21] I ask you to remember the saying of John, where he says that as Christ has laid down His life for us, to redeem us, so also He commands us to lay down our lives for

21 Greek: σκληρὸς οὗτος ὁ λόγος (John 6:60).

our brothers (1 John 3:[16]). Nor are our people doing anything else right now than risking their lives and all they have for the sake of their brothers, just as much as for themselves. And there are some who really do acknowledge this kindness of our people toward them, since by the little garrison of this city, as it were, they are still moderately safe from what could be the most extreme tyranny.

But our besiegers themselves owe a good part of their peace and fortune to the few who still stand with us in true piety and freedom. If these, too, are subjugated, will they not feel the eagle's talons in their feathers even more quickly than we?

The third aspect of Christian duty arises from the last one. Once supplication has been rendered ineffective, after Christians have made their confession and have insisted on their duty to protect the innocent against unjust persecution, it remains for them to do for the protection of Christ the very things the enemies are insisting on doing for the destruction of Christ, or at least to do something. Indeed, those who are able owe to us the same fidelity that Jonathan and Hushai paid to David when he was suffering injury from King Saul and from his son Absalom (1 Samuel 20; 2 Samuel 17). |They will help us not a little, together with the entire church of the faithful, by giving us timely warnings and by impeding the various plans of the Ahithophels who rise up against us.

Finally, let us say a little more about our duty to advance God's glory and the salvation of all people. Think, we beg you, all churches, and especially you leaders in them, you who do not want to knowingly betray and crucify Christ, think now how faithless your actions are, that you are not only abandoning us in our time of need, your own brothers and members of the same body of Christ, but also deserting the true religion and the Lord Christ Himself, so long as you do not openly oppose the papistic, interimistic, and adiaphoristic wolves in fear that you might suffer some harm.

You do not think this conflict has anything to do with you. So you look on idly for the sake of enjoying your own peace and pleasures. Or is the damage that has been done—or, rather, that is even now being done—not enough to show you how beautifully you have been thinking, in part that you have been silent while your brothers were in danger, and in part that you have helped the godless to inflict this calamity upon them? You must allow yourselves finally to come to your senses, even if only after you have been struck, and to be taught your duty, even if only by the outcome, which is the teacher of fools.

Thus all the faithful ought to be affected in common by this crisis, as if their own members were being cut off, or as if devils from hell were in wait even now to snatch their souls down to eternal destruction, because this is exactly what is happening so long as the true religion is being ripped away from them through so many lies and such great violence.

Nor do we intend to allow our spirits to be broken and to descend so quickly to the point of total despair, not for these comparatively insignificant calamities. For what particularly marks true courage, the kind Christians ought especially to possess, is not to despair of God's salvation even in the greatest misfortunes. Indeed, we know that it is God's way to lead His church down to hell so that He may takes pains to lead them up from it (1 Samuel 2:[6–8]). Affliction likes to begin in the house of the Lord and then finally to have its end with the wicked (1 Peter 4:[17]). We do not know when the end of these afflictions will come, how long God will allow the wicked to rage against us.

Very often He waits till things have come to the point of desperation and the battle appears lost before He comes to save in miraculous ways. So He saved Jerusalem with a miraculous event, when all the territory around them had already been overturned (2 Kings 19).[22] He saved the city of Bethulia when she sat in deepest desperation (Judith 7).[23] So also with Samaria (2 Kings 7).[24] More often still, He saves an entire people, as when He led His people out of Egypt.[25]

Therefore, we should not despair of the almighty power of our God nor imagine that because we are weak His strength has also been diminished and His hand cut short. This cowardice of ours is a great crime. Heathen, who knew nothing certain about God, about the immortality of the soul, about eternal life, often met death for the sake

22 In the time of Hezekiah, the Lord sent an angel to slay 185,000 of the Assyrian soldiers who were besieging Jerusalem. This caused the Assyrian king Sennacherib to return to Nineveh, where he was assassinated by his sons.

23 The apocryphal book of Judith tells how the beautiful Jewish widow Judith used her charm to trick and kill an Assyrian general who was besieging her city of Bethulia.

24 In the time of Elisha, an army of angels blinded an invading Syrian army, who were then led captive to Samaria. See 2 Kings 6:8–22.

25 The marginalia note that the salvation of the entire nation of Israel is seen in Exodus, Joshua, and Judges.

of political causes far more bravely than we Christians are willing to do for the true religion of Christ. ¦Shame on us! What delicate martyrs we are! I will stop short of saying Epicurean bellies.[26]

Therefore, let us all individually and with a brave heart do our duty in this most holy cause of preserving the true religion—teachers by teaching, magistrates by wielding the sword, subjects by promptly obeying their rulers when they command what is godly. For this is most certain, both that we have the true religion and that we can do nothing more saintly than to labor for its preservation and expose our lives to the utmost danger for it, each one according to his place and station in life, without confusion. For it is the preservation of true religion that especially magnifies God's glory and particularly preserves the salvation of our neighbor. So there is nothing we can do more pleasing to God, nothing more useful for our neighbor, than to promote and preserve true religion.

Here we should fix the following saying firmly in our souls and meditate on it honestly. Although spoken by a heathen, it is perfectly worthy of a Christian and confirmed everywhere in Holy Scripture: "Death is the end of life for all men, even if you were to lock yourself in the most fortified tower."[27]

Upstanding men should always act honestly, hope for good, and bear bravely whatever God gives. We should be completely subject to God, eagerly do what He commands, and leave the outcome to Him. We have a sure promise that the labor we undertake according to His Word will not be in vain but will bear its fruit.[28] ¦It is certain that Christ is with His church and will defend her to the end even against all the gates of hell.[29]

But as regards us individually, it is not so certain that we will escape the present perils of this life. We must all individually be conformed to the Son of God in this world and through various afflictions, and

---

26 Cf. Philippians 3:19 (ESV): "Their god is their belly."

27 Demosthenes (384–322 BC), *On the Crown*, 97: "The end of life to all men is death, even if he keeps himself guarded in a closet." The saying is quoted also in Lucian of Samosata (ca. 120–ca. 180), *Encomium of Demosthenes*, 5.

28 1 Corinthians 15:58 (ESV): "Therefore, my beloved brothers, be steadfast, immovable, always abounding in the work of the Lord, knowing that in the Lord your labor is not in vain."

29 Cf. Matthew 28:20; 16:18.

finally, through death itself, enter into eternal life.[30] But we have this most certain promise, that whether we live or we die we are the Lord's, and that the momentary afflictions of the present life are furnishing for us a weight of eternal glory beyond compare (Romans 14:[8]; 2 Corinthians 4:[17–18]).

Let us therefore do what God commands us in holding to true religion, each one in his own place, with the greatest diligence, convinced that we were not born simply for this miserable and short life, but to hasten as sojourners through this life to another, as on a journey. Let us be convinced that in that other life we will without doubt be most blessed forever. Although here on earth every evil be spoken against us on account of the name of the Lord (Matthew 5:[11–12], and though we suffer every injustice, we will certainly receive a hundredfold and possess eternal life with Christ our Lord and all the saints.[31]

It remains for all of us to pray together to the God and Father of our Lord Jesus Christ, that He Himself preserve us in the true confession of His Son and in all the duties which demand confession from us; that He not allow us to be drawn away from these duties or conquered by apathy, cowardice, false wisdom, or any allurements of this world. May our heavenly Father so govern the outcome of these dangerous events to the benefit of us all, so that the Antichrist cannot triumph with his father, the devil, against Christ, nor the people of the Antichrist mock the people of Christ and say, "Where is your God?" "Where is your Gospel?" Come, then, Lord Jesus! Come and redeem us for the glory of Your name! |"Indeed, I am coming," He says. "I am coming quickly. For I will not give My glory to another, nor shall the gates of the world or of hell prevail against My church. Heaven and earth will pass away, but My words will never pass way."[32] Praise be to Christ, our eternal King. He lives, and so we will live. We will be glorified with Him, as we also suffer with Him and are killed for His sake all the day.[33]

AMEN.

30 Cf. Acts 14:22.

31 Cf. Mark 10:30.

32 This is a catena of Bible verses, cited in the marginalia, including Revelation 22:20; Isaiah 42:8; Matthew 16:18; Luke 21:33; John 14:19; Romans 8:17.

33 Psalm 44:22; Romans 8:36.

Nicolaus Amsdorf, subscribed with his own hand.
Nikolaus Gallus, pastor at the Church of St. Udalric
Lucas Rosenthal, pastor at the Church of St. John
Johann Stengel, pastor at the Church of St. James
Henning Freden, pastor at the Church of St. Catharine
Ambrose Hitfeld, pastor at the Church of St. Peter
Johann Baumgarten, pastor at the Church of the Holy Spirit
Joachim Wolterstorp, pastor in the Southern Citadel
Henrich Gercken, pastor in the New City
The individual pastors have subscribed with their own hands, in their own name and in the name of other ministers.

POSTSCRIPT

ON April 13, Master Stephen Tucher, our most faithful colleague in the Gospel of Christ at the Church of St. Udalric, departed from this life in the confession of the true faith and in prayer to the Son of God. He died a very peaceful death, but we miss him terribly. His learning was excellent, as was his skill in judgment and his passion for true piety. His zeal was ardent, surpassing that of many. And his soul was completely devoid of that Epicurean apathy which leads many to think the present battles over religion unimportant or irrelevant to their personal lives. His virtues are clear and well attested by many witnesses, both privately and publicly.

When we came to visit him as he struggled with his sickness, some of us heard him very firmly and indignantly condemn the deceits of the Interimists and Adiaphorists. He did this often, but especially in the last few days before his death, just as he had done much earlier in his public writing, which served as the preface to the commentary of the man of God, Dr. Martin Luther on Isaiah 53.[1] Also to a sermon of Luther edited by him.[2] They heard him also exhort us to persevere in this our true confession against the contagion of that Pharisaical leaven[3] and say many other things with all seriousness pertaining to this matter. These, perhaps, will be published by others in their own place.

Among other things, he asked that when this our little book should be published, if we were willing, to add his name here and testify to the church that he died in the confession of that faith which this book contains.

1 This was a reprint from Michael Lotter's press in Magdeburg, with a preface by Tucher included. See *Enarratio 53. Capitis Esaiae prophetae* (Lotter, 1550).

2 Reprinted in Magdeburg with a preface by Tucher.

3 Cf. Matthew 16:6.

Therefore, as godly men, in order to fulfill his godly request, we have written these things about his resolution, and all the more willingly because we judge that this will greatly help the rest of the church to strengthen our resolution and give glory to Christ. For when a dying man calls on the judgment of God and is not confounded in doing so, so that according to Christ's word he neither saw nor tasted death,[4] that is a great witness to the truth and to a good conscience.

[Psalm 93]
The Lord reigns. He has put on majesty.
The Lord has put on strength and girded Himself.
For He has established the world, which will not be moved.
Your throne has been established from that time;
You are from everlasting.

The rivers have lifted up, O Lord,
the rivers have lifted up their voice.
The rivers have lifted up their waves,
from the voices of many waters.
The rising of the sea is marvelous;
marvelous is the Lord on high.

Your testimonies have been made exceedingly sure.
Holiness befits Your house,
O Lord, for length of days.

4 John 8:51.

SUBJECT INDEX

SCRIPTURE INDEX